YORKSHIRE'S MURDEROUS WOMEN

FOUL DEEDS AND SUSPICIOUS DEATHS Series

Wharncliffe's *Foul Deeds and Suspicious Deaths* series explores, in detail, crimes of passion, brutal murders and foul misdemeanours from early modern times to the present day. Victorian street crime, mysterious deaths and modern murders tell tales where passion, jealousy and social deprivation brought unexpected violence to those involved. From unexplained death and suicide to murder and manslaughter, the books provide a fascinating insight into the lives of both victims and perpetrators as well as society as a whole.

Other titles in the series include:

Foul Deeds and Suspicious Deaths in Bolton, Glynis Cooper
ISBN: 1-903425-63-8. £9.99

Foul Deeds and Suspicious Deaths in London's East End, Geoffrey Howse
ISBN: 1-903425-71-9. £10.99

Foul Deeds and Suspicious Deaths in & around Durham, Maureen Anderson
ISBN: 1-903425-46-8. £9.99

Foul Deeds and Suspicious Deaths in Hampstead, Holburn & St Pancras, Mark Aston
ISBN: 1-903425-94-8. £10.99

Foul Deeds and Suspicious Deaths in Colchester, Patrick Denney
ISBN: 1-903425-80-8. £10.99

Foul Deeds and Suspicious Deaths in Newport, Terry Underwood
ISBN: 1-903425-59-X. £9.99

Foul Deeds and Suspicious Deaths Around Derby, Kevin Turton
ISBN: 1-903425-76-X. £9.99

Foul Deeds and Suspicious Deaths in and Around Scunthorpe, Stephen Wade
ISBN: 1-903425-88-3. £9.99

More Foul Deeds and Suspicious Deaths in Wakefield, Kate Taylor
ISBN: 1-903425-48-4. £9.99

Foul Deeds and Suspicious Deaths in York, Keith Henson
ISBN: 1-903425-33-6. £9.99

Foul Deeds and Suspicious Deaths on the Yorkshire Coast, Alan Whitworth
ISBN: 1-903425-01-8. £9.99

Foul Deeds and Suspicious Deaths in Coventry, David McGrory
ISBN: 1-903425-57-3. £9.99

Foul Deeds and Suspicious Deaths in Manchester, Martin Baggoley
ISBN: 1-903425-65-4. £9.99

Foul Deeds and Suspicious Deaths in Newcastle, Maureen Anderson
ISBN: 1-903425-34-4. £9.99

Foul Deeds and Suspicious Deaths in Hull, David Goodman
ISBN: 1-903425-43-3. £9.99

Foul Deeds and Suspicious Deaths Around Newport, Terry Underwood
ISBN: 1-903425-59-X. £9.99

Please contact us via any of the methods below for more information or a catalogue.
WHARNCLIFFE BOOKS
47 Church Street – Barnsley – South Yorkshire S70 2AS
Tel: 01226 734555 – 734222; Fax: 01226 724438
E-mail: enquiries@pen-and-sword.co.uk
Website: www.wharncliffebooks.co.uk

Kirklees
METROPOLITAN·COUNCIL
CULTURAL SERVICES

Culture + Leisure Services
Red Doles Lane
Huddersfield, West Yorks. HD21YF

**THIS BOOK SHOULD BE RETURNED ON OR BEFORE THE LATEST
DATE STAMPED BELOW.
FINES ARE CHARGED IF THE ITEM IS LATE.**

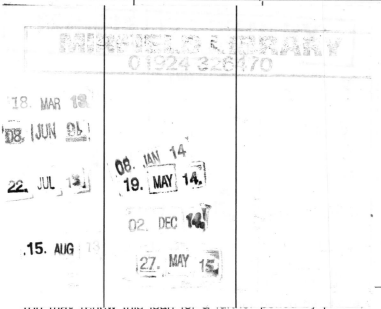
You may renew this loan for a further period by post,
letter, personal visit or at www.kirklees.gov.uk/libraries,
provided that the book is not required by another reader.

NO MORE THAN THREE RENEWALS ARE PERMITTED

W72

Yorkshire's Murderous Women

More than two centuries of killings

STEPHEN WADE

Wharncliffe Books

First published in Great Britain in 2007 by
Wharncliffe Books
an imprint of
Pen and Sword Books Ltd
47 Church Street
Barnsley
South Yorkshire
S70 2AS

© Stephen Wade 2007

ISBN: 978-1-84563-023-2

Typeset in 11/13pt Plantin by Concept, Huddersfield.

Printed and bound in England by Biddles.

Pen and Sword Books Ltd incorporates the Imprints of
Pen & Sword Aviation, Pen & Sword Maritime,
Pen & Sword Military, Wharncliffe Books,
Pen & Sword Select, Pen and Sword Military Classics
and Leo Cooper.

For a complete list of Pen & Sword titles please contact
PEN & SWORD BOOKS LIMITED
47 Church Street
Barnsley
South Yorkshire
S70 2BR
England
E-mail: enquiries@pen-and-sword.co.uk
Website: www.pen-and-sword.co.uk

Contents

Acknowledgements

This book has not been easy to research. Some of the Victorian cases are very obscure and there is sparse material at times. Reference libraries and archive staff have been very helpful. Staff at the Brynmor Jones Library, University of Hull and at County Hall, Beverley, have also been very helpful, particularly Lizzy Baker.

As many cases involve infanticide, some sources have been academic studies rather than primary material, and books by David Bentley and John Eccleston have been invaluable. Some stories have had to be handled with tact and sensitivity, notably the tragic account of the Castles in Driffield and the brief notes on Avril Gregory; the full story of the latter's offence has been told in *Killers* by Kate Kray. Although my main chapters end with the 1980 story of the Maws, I wanted to mention some more recent stories, albeit briefly, so these have been included in the final chapter, though in no depth.

There are also the related topics of feminist perspectives on crime and for this I needed some conversations with various writers and academics. I have tried to incorporate some of these contemporary lines of thought into the cases, notably in the inclusion of modern medical knowledge in the cases of child murder.

Acknowledgement is due to the *Hull Daily Mail* for the use of the pictures from the Hutchinson case and East Yorkshire Archives for the Long Riston case.

Introduction

A play called *And All the Children Cried*, written by Judith Jones, was staged at West Yorkshire Playhouse in 2002. It concerns the nature of women who kill. Undoubtedly, it was destined to upset people and to be unsatisfactory to some critics and reviewers. The reason for this is not hard to find: the subject of women with a murderous nature is sensitive, troubling and fraught with difficulties of interpretation. One reviewer at the time noted that 'The very presence of Myra Hindley, one of the most iconic and detested figures of popular imagination, means that it is hard to examine the issues through the glare of notoriety.' This was Charles Spencer, and he located perhaps the most enigmatic aspect of this most mythic department of true crime writing.

History shows us that there is nothing new in this. Some of the most notorious cases of women being tried for wilful murder in English history involve moral beliefs and ideologies of power that are impossible to accept today. Something profound in the human mind and in the sense of moral community feels an extraordinary revulsion at the thought of a woman taking a life. Until 1827, a woman who took the life of her husband was committing, not murder, but petty treason. Until 1790, this earned a punishment of burning at the stake rather than hanging. When a woman was hanged for 'husband murder', even as late as 1825, the ritual in the official execution was very different from that of a male killer, as this account of the death of Hannah Read shows:

A bed or mattress was placed upon the sledge, which was drawn by a horse, upon which the prisoner was secured by a rope. On reaching the Bridewell, she was carried into the gaoler's house ... About eleven o'clock she was again placed upon the sledge, and was drawn along the gaol yard to the foot of the steps leading to the scaffold; soon after she appeared on the platform followed by the High Sheriff and the usual attendants ... She seemed earnest in supplicating mercy for her sins and invoking the divine favour on her unfortunate children and relatives . . . (The Times, 9 August 1825)

Hannah Read had a very different experience from that of the average male murderer. Her crime was also a more extreme form of sin and a more outrageous offence against the social and religious hierarchy on earth.

But many of the stories in this book come from the period when the majority of killings by women were those of infanticide. The press reports of the alarmingly common cases of attempted suicide and infanticide are desperately sad, as in this typical one from 1850:

Mary Hardwick, a miserable – looking creature, was indicted for attempting to murder her child. On the Saturday preceding she was seen standing with a child in her arms near the Brighton custom-house, when she suddenly ran down to the sea, threw the child into the water, and then jumped in herself. The woman and child were dragged out in a state of insensibility . . .

When the poor woman recovered, her husband reviled her and 'expressed a wish that she had drowned herself'. Note that 'murder her child' was emphasised in this report from Dickens' journal, *Household Narrative*. In the Victorian period, this kind of tragic attempt at suicide was counterbalanced in the unsound morality of the time with the case of affiliation. That is, attempts to kill the children of immoral unions in order to avoid being a 'fallen woman' were rife; but what about the male transgressors?

A case from Dewsbury in 1850 shows this, as here a man of the cloth, Reverend Stephen Matthews, was in the dock. This vicar of Hanging Heaton stood accused of being the father of an illegitimate child born to Mary Hellewell (sixteen-years-old). The court now found, as this was a retrial, that 'criminal intercourse had continued for two years.' The magistrates declined to make an order of affiliation, which would have tied the churchman to a regular maintenance payment for the upkeep and education of his child. Such affiliation hearings were rare.

In most instances, the chosen means of murder by women was poison. In 1850, a report stated that the number of people tried for murder by poison between 1839 and 1849 was 154. Of these, sixty-nine were men and eighty-five were female. The notorious nineteenth century cases of Florence Maybrick (Liverpool) and Priscilla Biggadyke (Lincolnshire), together with the mystery of Florence Bravo, have perhaps made the poison narrative familiar to readers. Typically this is a situation of adulterous love or 'the worm turning' after maltreatment; then a slow and steady administering of arsenic takes place, and finally the death of the man leads to suspicions. In working class households, this was often in terms of arsenic being soaked from fly-papers.

But poison stories and women killers are always complicated by the popularity of arsenic and other poisons being taken in very small doses by men, with the aim of enhancing their sexual potency. James Maybrick in Liverpool (once a Ripper suspect) was one such addict. Most Yorkshire cases are in the settings of the urban poor.

The scenario in Yorkshire during the Industrial Revolution is one involving, as a rule, a woman with a large family and a violent drunken husband or partner. The pressures of work, poverty and drink combine to make life intolerable with a man who abuses his woman, and so poison becomes the best method of removing him from the scene. These lifestyles of deprivation and stress also account for the related high incidence of suicide in this period. As Katherine Watson has written: '. . . there is a clear difference in intent between suicide and attempted murder-suicide, the latter being the crime of which most mentally unstable poisoners were guilty'. She adds that three-quarters of the suicide-poisoners were female in the 1860s when some statistics were available.

Petty treason is surely the most revolting concept in law, underlying some of these Yorkshire stories. Burning at the stake for petty treason was abolished on 5 June 1790. A woman sentenced to be burnt for this crime was treated incredibly cruelly and barbarously. The worst that could happen was the fate that befell Catherine Hayes who, in 1726, was to be burned for killing her husband but 'her fire was lit before she was deprived of sensation by strangling' as the *Gloucester Journal* reported at the time. There was terrible discrimination in the concept; back in 1352 women were singled out for murder of spouses, along with servants who killed their masters, for the fate of burning at the stake, in the Statute of Treasons.

What this subject generally comes down to is that women killers are 'mad or bad.' At the heart of this, and important in many of the following cases, is the uneasy mix of sexuality and morality. As Shani D'Cruze (see Bibliography) has written: '... not only will a woman who has murdered often be identified as sexually deviant, but also a sexually transgressive woman will be all the more readily accepted as capable of murder'.

In 1487, two Dominicans, Heinrich Kramer and Jacob Sprenger, published *Malleus Maleficarum,* the tract that made a huge impact on the pursuit and persecution of women who were supposed witches. The witch craze across Europe in particular periods within the time-span of the fifteenth to the seventeenth centuries, had its impact in Yorkshire, as it did almost everywhere else. This was certainly increased in its intensity by King James I's book *Demonologie,* published following his participation in Scotland's most notorious witch-hunt in the years 1590–91. In Yorkshire, as James Sharpe has shown, there were witch accusations across the county, perhaps not always concerned with murder; but Agnes Walker of Warley near Halifax was accused of killing Richard Stanfeild, as recounted in my first chapter. More often, the witch stories meant that ordinary people had to go to court to struggle against defamation.

Of course, these stories will involve accounts of hangings, and this means that there are cases in which a man has to hang a woman. In the annals of the English hangmen, their accounts of hanging women are notably harrowing and emotional, as when James Berry had to hang Mary Lefley in Lincolnshire, or when John Ellis had to hang Edith Thompson. Ellis had also hanged Emily Swann in Leeds, but in the case of Thompson he wrote: 'It was agonising to see her held up by the four men, her bound feet on the trap-doors ...' Tennyson perhaps expressed the knotty morality at the heart of legal execution in his poem, *Rizpah,* in which he gives us the female stance on a hanging: 'Full of compassion and mercy – long suffering / oh yes, yes! / For the lawyer is born but to murder / the Saviour lives but to bless'. The lines are spoken by the mother of a young man who is hanged.

Finally, what of the crime of passion, the *crime passionel*? The thinking behind that always raises interesting comparisons when we look at murder cases in Britain. As Oliver Cyriax defines it in layman's form, this '. . . disposing of one's lover or spouse in a fit of passion . . . can constitute a defence to the charge of murder'. This is only in France, of course. But it has to be said that in recent times, the notion of a 'slow burn' motivation has gained more attention, largely owing to re-investigations of the execution of Ruth Ellis in 1955. Some Yorkshire stories of women killers invite a certain level of comparison, but in the nineteenth century the most prominent struggles in court in which defences were steadily assembled were those of insanity and provocation. Feminist issues, sadly, had to wait a long time to take centre stage in this respect. Traditional folklore and superstition has given us such a massive body of song, oral testimony and street literature in which women criminals are demonised that it will take a major cultural shift of perceptions to change attitudes. Typical of street poetry is the traditional rhyme, *Mary Arnold the Female Monster*, with its refrain:

This wretched woman's dreadful deed
does everyone affright.
With black beetle sin walnut shells
She deprived her child of sight.

In the beliefs and prejudices behind those lines we have the basis of the irrational set of beliefs in the communal foundations of the following case studies.

The question of legend cannot go unnoticed either, in a book aiming to cover the long centuries of Yorkshire history, so once again the thorny subject of Robin Hood and whether or not he was killed at Kirklees Priory by Elizabeth de Staynton has had to be confronted here. After all, folklore has a habit of creeping into the historical record of crime, as in the case of Mary Bateman's tongue. For that, see Chapter 8.

Part One

Between History and Folklore

CHAPTER 1

Witch Stories

She was said to have willed the death of the master of Kippax Hall . . .

An account of women murderers in Yorkshire has to begin with early tales, some of them utter mythology and urban myth, but these cases – witch fever accusations – often went to the courts, and so they became a part of the county's legal and criminal history. The familiar scene is of a man having bad luck with his animals on the farm or always being subject to having ailing children, and then a local woman who had previously been seen as 'a cunning person' escalated to the condition of witch.

Anyone trying to tell actual murder stories involving witchcraft is in for a challenge. In Yorkshire one of the difficulties is the number of wild and tall tales surrounding many women who were somewhere in between witches and general village quacks and advisers, such as the Ling-Bob witch, Hannah Green, who died rich in 1810. The middle classes paid her visits to help in retrieving lost treasures and such was the strength of the myth surrounding her that it was said that she could only be killed by being shot with a silver bullet.

Unfortunately, this tale from popular cultural history was not always merely an old wives' tale and nipped in the bud. The reference works and websites devoted to the history of witchcraft in Europe provide us with an alarmingly long list of persons executed for witchcraft.

Having said that, it is not an easy matter to find a female witch in Yorkshire who certainly did bring about the death of her victim; but the most famous witch in the region is surely Mother Shipton, who was concerned with prophecy and would have been known simply as a 'cunning person' – figures that were popular well into the nineteenth century. She was thought of as a clever scholar and, according to one account, 'caused

Mother Shipton, witch and prophet, from an old print. Author's collection

hatred and envy in her colleagues'. One candidate for a real killing is possibly Mary Pannel, burned in 1603 for allegedly bringing about the death of the master of Kippax Hall. That oral traditional tale was handed down and was recorded by a member of a Devon history society, taken from her grandmother. Yet we know little more than this, other than that a field and a hill in the area are still known as Mary Pannel Hill and Mary Pannel Field. We know she was tried at York by a grand jury.

A case from Warley, near Halifax, is more detailed. This is the story of Agnes Walker of that village, who in 1598 was supposedly the killer of a local man, Richard Stanfeild of Sowerby Bridge. Warley is the small suburb of Halifax that the driver encounters as he travels from King Cross on the small road parallel to the Lancashire Road. It is not difficult to imagine the isolation here in the sixteenth century, when ignorance of medicine was as widespread and dangerous as the absence of basic learning. Poor Agnes, a widow, was convicted of Stanfeild's death, against whom she was supposed to have applied the 'diabolical arts' of sorcery.

The victim is said to have languished from August 1598 to January 1599 and Agnes was alleged to have 'killed and slew' him. The statute of 5 Elizabeth c.16 (known as the Statute of Witchcraft) made this possible – at least in the popular imagination. This was 'an act against conjurations, enchantments and witchcrafts' and one part of this states: '... every such offender in invocations or conjurations as is aforesaid, their counsellors and aiders, as also every such offender in witchcraft, enchantment, charm or sorcery, whereby the death of any person does ensue ... shall suffer pains of death as felons and shall lose the privilege of benefit of clergy'.

It may have been the case that Mr Stanfeild had any one of a number of illnesses of which we now know a great deal. Therefore, in this Yorkshire 'murder' we have to use the word rather carefully and with a large amount of scepticism and disbelief.

More commonly, a witch tale was in the courts because the resulting local notoriety lead to a defamation suit. In 1617, in Burley, Leeds, a dispute arose between Thomas Brooke and the Beaumonds, John and Isabel. The matter came to an open challenge to a fight outside Beaumond's house. But the most telling part of the account is the testimony of one Ann Snowden of Bramley, who was working as a servant to a Bramley man and who knew the Beaumonds. She said that Thomas Brooke walked past her in the fields and told her that Isabel Beaumond

Knaresborough in the early twentieth century, close to Mother Shipton's cave. The author

had bewitched his cattle. Snowden simply stated that Isabel was an honest woman.

Historians still have a lot to do in developing an understanding of the witch crazes throughout our history. As James Sharpe has written: 'we need to develop a fully gendered interpretation of witchcraft and witch beliefs'. In early modern Yorkshire, stories and court cases were rife, and major stories did touch the county, such as when one of the infamous Pendle witches was brought across the border to be tried at York.

However, until recent times, stories of witches were passed on through the generations, as J Fairfax Blakeborough, the writer on Yorkshire history, has recalled:

> *Yet at the dawn of this century we have talked with old men, who in hushed tones, and with the fullest conviction, told of the spells, curses and machinations of local witches. We listened to stories of the marvellous power of the 'wisemen' who could circumvent the black art.*

Somewhere in that oral history are perhaps well-documented attempts, and indeed successes, in committing murder by these occult means. In chapter seven, with the life of Mary Bateman, we have the most well documented example, but for the earlier times, too much superstition and folklore gets in the way of actual criminal records.

CHAPTER 2

Was Robin Slain by Elizabeth?

He was buried as a robber and an outlaw of the peace of the church.

In the late Victorian years, the popular periodicals were keen to perpetuate the Robin Hood myth, but there was, and still is, a need to find out exactly who the outlaw was behind that legend. One of the most popular antiquarian journals of the 1890s, featured an item on Kirklees Park, near Hartshead, the supposed burial place of Robin. The writer says, with reference to Ritson, the great historian of folklore: 'Ritson says that Robin Hood was born in Loxley ... his extraction being noble ... Without entering into the history of his life, we may speak of his resting place, which is situated in a retired spot on the border of a wood ...' The author appears anxious to seem well informed, yet his piece is vague and never really faces the questions of any documentation about the killing of Robin Hood in that place.

A number of historians are convinced that not only was he killed there at Kirklees, but also that he was murdered by the prioress of the priory, who was Elizabeth de Staynton. The old *Gest of Robin Hood* from late medieval times has what one writer calls 'the treacherous killing of a martial hero in sleazy domestic circumstances'. One has to agree that this has some feeling of substance in it. There is a strong tradition that Robin lived at Wakefield, and that is near enough to Kirklees to fit well with this tradition.

But did Elizabeth kill Robin? The beginning of this is in the old ballad, *The Death of Robin Hood* from a first text found in 1786, though much older. This poem contains the element of Robin firing an arrow at the priory, to mark the spot where he will have to stop and have help, for he is badly wounded. The

Robin Hood's Grave, from a Victorian magazine. Author's collection

tradition here is that the prioress was a relative: 'But I have a cousin lives down below.' He says that he will be safe there:

> *The dame prior is my aunt's daughter*
> *and nie unto my kinne;*
> *I know she would do me no harme this day,*
> *For all the world to winne.*

But in the poem, she bleeds him until he is virtually dead:

> *She laid the blood-irons to Robin's vain . . .*
> *and well then wist good Robin Hood*
> *treason was within.*

What had supposed to have happened is that she lets some blood, ostensibly to treat him for his feverous condition, but she over-bleeds him and he is very weak. Then she calls for the villain 'Red Roger' who finishes Robin off. One view of this is that there is religious symbolism at work, and A J Pollard puts it this way:

> *The prioress has been transformed into a widow. To some extent it would make more sense if Robin's nemesis had been a widow who had taken a vow of chastity, but broken these with her*

ROBIN HOOD:

A

COLLECTION

Of all the Ancient

POEMS, SONGS, AND BALLADS,

NOW EXTANT,

RELATIVE TO THAT CELEBRATED

𝔈𝔫𝔤𝔩𝔦𝔰𝔥 𝔒𝔲𝔱𝔩𝔞𝔴:

To which are prefixed

HISTORICAL ANECDOTES OF HIS LIFE.

LONDON:

PRINTED FOR C. STOCKING, 3, PATERNOSTER-ROW,
By J. and C. Adlard, Bartholomew-close.

1823.

Title page for a Robin Hood anthology. Author's collection

accomplice. Be that as it may, the short version clearly identifies
his betrayer as the prioress.

There appears to be some substance in the details of the tale,
including the evil Roger. This is said to be Roger of Doncaster
(spelt 'Donkesly' in the first version). Research suggests that
he was from Sprotborough, and the references to him in the
fourteenth century are interesting since he has a link with
Sherwood, as he owned land there.

The events in question, then, took place in 1347, when Robin
fired the arrow, his last shot, and said he was to be buried where
the arrow fell to ground. But the suspect in question is not
necessarily the killer. As Barbara Green has convincingly
shown, if the date of the death is 1347, not 1247 as in some
traditions, then, as on the tomb, the prioress at the time was
Mary Startin, not Elizabeth de Staynton. As Barbara has
pointed out, we need a motive, and the only one suggested is
that Robin opposed ecclesiastical corruption, as graphically described by Chaucer in his *Pardoner's Tale* (written about fifty
years after these events). We have to say that it was a nasty and
slow method of killing, if indeed it was so. There is plenty of
mystery in the bare facts, without recourse to the wilder
theories.

Whoever she was, the woman let the hero's blood so much
that he died, and surely she has to be one of the first Yorkshire
women murderers. Robin died nobly, though, with these supposed words:

Let me have length and breadth enough
With under my head a green sod;
That they may say, when I am dead,
Here lies bold Robin Hood.

Part Two
Murder Casebook

CHAPTER 3

Threesome Problems: Elizabeth Broadingham 1776

Some ghoulish witnesses collected her ashes as souvenirs . . .

Over the centuries, York Castle has witnessed some terrible scenes of human suffering, but few can equal the story of Elizabeth Broadingham. The narrative vaguely echoes the actions of Lady Macbeth (lacking the 'milk of human kindness') except that the setting and the motives are the lowest and most despicable imaginable.

John Broadingham, her husband, was not exactly a pillar of the community. He was locked away in York dungeons for robbery when Elizabeth began her affair with Thomas Aikney, a man younger than she. It was a case of extreme passion, 'while the cat's away', and she liked the pleasures of loving and sex with the other man so much that she moved in with him.

A man coming out of prison after all kinds of deprivations expects some comfort and loyalty from his family. John Broadingham found none of this; he merely found that his wife had left the home. Elizabeth appears to have wanted more than simply living with Aikney as his partner; she wanted to be free of the marriage with John, and to remove the husband from the scene altogether was her aim.

She began to work on Aikney with a view to leading him into the murder of John. The younger man at first resisted these pleas and wiles, but after some time he began to be influenced. It is recounted, though not definitely known, that Elizabeth made sure that Aikney had plenty of alcohol in him and tempted him in all the ways she could invent, as she allured him into a murderous pact. He finally went along with the plan.

An execution, from old print. Author's collection

Elizabeth must have been a very influential speaker and something of an actress; not only had she inveigled her way into Aikney's life, she now played the part of good wife, returning to John and apparently wanting to return to the marital harmony they once had. John took her back. But only a week or so after moving back home, she was talking to Thomas Aikney about their plan, and sorting out the details of where and when it would be done. Her lover still vainly tried to resist, but Elizabeth was relentless. Poor Thomas thought that the best move was to run away and avoid the confrontation, to make a new start elsewhere.

Things came to a head on the night of 8 February 1776, when Elizabeth woke her husband saying there was a loud noise downstairs. John staggered down to investigate and made his way to the door where Aikney was pounding on the wood. As John Broadingham opened up, Aikney knifed him in the chest and then, as the frenzied attack continued, he stabbed the man in the thigh and the leg. With the knife stuck in his belly, John managed to walk out into the street, where he was seen by neighbours. So badly was the husband hurt that he had almost been eviscerated in the assault; he was clutching his stomach and his guts were exposed. The report at the time states that he was 'supporting his bowels'.

John Broadingham died the day after the attack. It took only a short time for neighbours and magistrates to find Aikney and then the whole story was revealed. Elizabeth and Thomas confessed and he was hanged at York on 20 March. In this tale lies the incredible difference between punishment for murder and petty treason. Aikney's body, as was the custom, was cut down and then transported to Leeds Infirmary for use in dissection

Map of York by John Speed, 1611. Author's collection

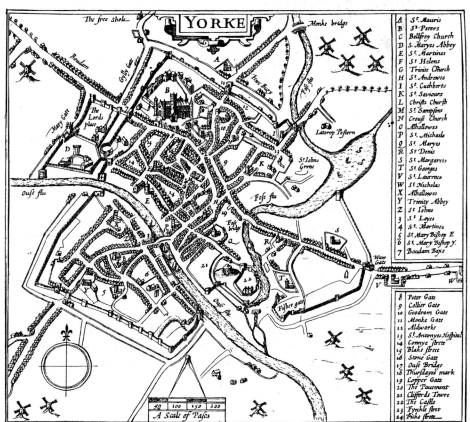

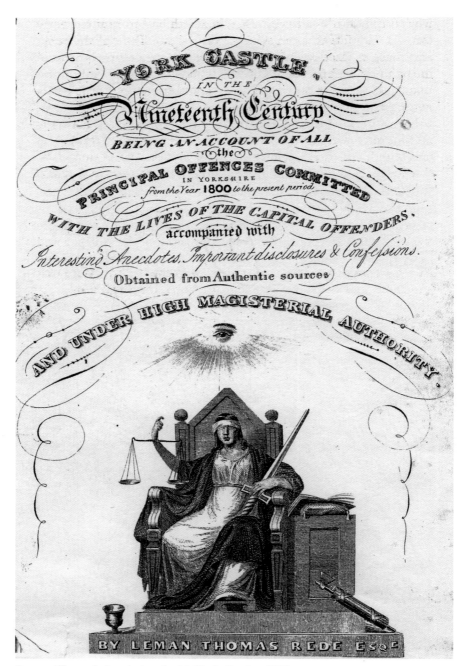

Leman Thomas's frontispiece for his York Castle, 1829. Author's collection

work for medical education. But Elizabeth had committed petty treason. Her fate was to be burnt at the stake. The only humane act in these cases was that the executioner normally strangled the woman before the fire was set alight, and he did so for Elizabeth. She was burnt and some ghoulish witnesses collected her ashes as souvenirs.

Mercy never entered into the matter when a woman was considered for the death penalty in the late eighteenth and early nineteenth centuries. The great journalist of the period, J W Robertson Scott, has a memory of a woman on a scaffold at this time:

> ... *it was an old woman, a mere old wrinkled, wretched bundle. She was said to have killed a bastard. She cried, "You cannot hang me!" But they did.*

Burning for petty treason, as explained in the introduction, was abolished in 1790 – too late for Elizabeth Broadingham.

CHAPTER 4

A Deadly Potion in Batley: Ann Scalbird
1794

Her death had been caused by a steady administering of arsenic . . .

It took Mary Scalbird six days to die. She been bed-ridden and suffered horrific agonies on each of those days, insisting all the way through that awful time that her daughter-in-law, Ann, had poisoned her. What this true? The only way to find out was to bring in the best medical men available. She had been attended in her dying by George Swinton, a Dewsbury surgeon, and he was the one who heard the woman making the accusations. No detail in this report hints at why this might have happened. How it was done is no mystery: arsenic was used around the home at the time for all kinds of purposes, mainly as a pesticide, and most homes had a problem with vermin. It was easily available at the time, as anyone could buy a quantity from a druggist, and these retailers were not to be effectively regulated until after the 1851 Arsenic Act.

Arsenic does not make for an easy death; when the most typical form, white oxide, was used, it causes a burning sensation in the victim's throat, and then there is repeated violent vomiting, with blood in the vomit. After that there are severe stomach pains, absolutely intolerable and akin to the feeling of extreme heat inside the body, too intense to cope with. Then there is muscle cramp and diarrhoea. The skin becomes blueish in hue before the final collapse.

The experienced doctors who attended Mrs Scalbird would have seen this familiar pattern of symptoms. Before there was an inquest, because of the suspicions aroused in Sykes's mind, a well respected doctor named Benjamin Sykes was called in to help. Sykes was a graduate of the highly regarded Guy's Hospital (founded in 1724) and he was well known and respected around the Wakefield area at the time. Sykes, who only had to travel from Gomersal, joined Swinton at the post-mortem. Sure enough, they both agreed that Mrs Scalbird had died from arsenical poisoning.

The long and painful dying was now explained fully and Ann was the one who had been responsible. The poor woman had had to endure this ordeal, with the doctor unable to help. Her death had been caused by a steady administering of arsenic, and medical expertise had pinpointed the cause, and so the finger pointed at Ann, who was convicted and executed for the crime.

The case is interesting because it helps us to understand how the law and the medical profession were trying to cope with the alarming rate of suspicious deaths apparently by poisoning, whether by accident, by wrong dosage, or by criminal intent. Local doctors would sometimes perform both the autopsy and then the analysis, in order that information and testimony would be available in court, rather than the instance of a surgeon or an apothecary merely signing a death certificate and writing down any one of a number of illnesses with symptoms similar to death by arsenic process. Another difficulty in detection was that, traditionally, autopsies would be performed on the table of the place of the death therefore expert pathology was out of the question, and there would be some haste in the matter.

It is not clear what Ann Scalbird's motive was, but one thing is certain: she chose the wrong place to do the deed. The work of Sykes in that area was outstanding and exceptional. It must be remembered that it was not until over thirty years after this case that any reliable chemical test was conceived and applied; these were the Marsh and Reinsch tests. Another factor by that time (certainly by the 1840s) was the arrival of the railways and the more manageable journeys that could be made by experts to travel to trials in order to give expert opinion.

CHAPTER 5

The Sad Tale of Mary Thorp 1800

The wretched girl became a miserable mother, and gave birth to a child whose smiles would become her reproach.

At York in 1800, Mary Thorp, just twenty-two-years-old, pleaded not guilty to a charge of 'murdering her male infant'. It was the first capital offence tried in Yorkshire in the new century. One of the very first accounts of the case, published in 1831, is retained and keeps back much of the material around the story, simply pointing out that Mary began domestic service at fourteen, was happy, and then was seduced 'by one, whilst he pretended to lead the confiding girl on to happiness, brought her to ruin, misery and disgrace'. It appears from the records that there was no knowledge of the identity of this man.

That course of seduction and ruin is arguably the typology of the infanticide chronicle throughout centuries of English history. In Mary Thorp's case the events were chillingly simple: a woman friend helped in the birth of the child, and then, according to one reporter, a week later Mary took the child to a pond and threw it into the water, a stone tied around its neck. This account appears to be too vague; she in fact stayed with a widow called Hartley in Sheffield, for the delivery, then said she was moving on to Derby to be with her sister. But her plan was to go to Ecclesfield. It was there, in the river near Bridge Houses, that the child was thrown to its death, with tape tied tightly around its neck.

The child had been strangled before it was thrown into the water, and there was no doubt that the tape around its neck was Mary's. Hartley identified the material. There was an inquest following this discovery, of course. The charge was murder, and the coroner arranged for Mary Thorp to stand trial at York. The opinion of a commentator at the time was simple but powerful: 'The wretched girl became a miserable mother, and gave birth to a child whose smiles became her reproach.'

The defence was that Mary Thorp was not aware of what she was doing and was delirious. The medical men agreed that she had indeed suffered from 'milk fever' but that this was not sufficient cause of any palpable insanity in Mary. She had apparently intended to do the deed, and did so with awareness of the act. In spite of the fact that she did not look like a ragged victim of street poverty and likely immorality, the jury was not sympathetic, and took into consideration the circumstantial evidence, along with the point about no real insanity in Mary, and so reached a verdict of guilty.

When the sentence was passed, as reported by Thomas Rede Leman, Mary 'bore it with great firmness and curtseyed very lowly to the court before she left it'. At the York Tyburn on 17 March she was hanged.

According to the first full report, the morality fixed as part of the judgement on Mary was entirely in keeping with the limited understanding of infanticide at the time: 'In a case like this, there can be no medium between pity for the offender, or utter abhorrence' yet the writer goes on to tackle the subject of her possible temporary insanity:

> *Medical experience tells us that fevers of all descriptions affect the sanity of the sufferer: milk fever is most powerful in its effects; and though the law might condemn, society may pity such a criminal.*

It is a sad story indeed. Mary in court was a 'pale and care-worn creature' and of course, she had been the subject of a heartless seduction. This pattern of behaviour, leading to child murder, was to preoccupy the best minds of the later Victorian period. Elizabeth Gaskell wrote her novel, *Ruth*, in 1853, to deal with the difficult subject of the seduction of a poor working girl by a rich man. She lost friends over the publication.

In cases like that of Mary Thorp, then, the commentaries show a great deal of sympathy, and writers were clearly aware of the clash between criminal law and moral opinion. But all this was of no use to the condemned young woman, destined to die

A popular advert for 'women's weakness', c.1920. Author's collection

on the scaffold. We have to admire her resolve and self-control. When the verdict was given she stood firm, and it was noted that 'In person she was extremely prepossessing.' It has to be said, with a more modern understanding of the dynamics of a courtroom, that she should have been less prepossessing and more frail and demure. It might have had some influence on those in judgement.

CHAPTER 6

A Domestic Tragedy: Mary Chapel 1802

I am a wretched woman. It was my child; I never meant it harm ...

ary Chapel was just nineteen, and in the domestic service of Colonel Surtees at Ackland, when she faced the judge and jury at York on a charge of infanticide: a similar predicament to that of Mary Thorp. Chapel's story is, however, unlike Thorp's in one important respect – that she and the father were in love, and only parted because of the exigencies of hard times.

Mary courted a young man who was also in service, but as a contemporary account puts it: 'The young man to whom we have alluded became careless of his duties, excited reprehension and resolved at length, in that tumultuous year 1801, to take refuge in the army.' The sequence of events that led to Mary's downfall is the material of literary tragedy. She and the young man walked out together and went to a local feast; her man had begged her to take some time off work for that. They had a good time, and of course, it was a rare opportunity for them to make love. Sure enough, that one fateful union led to her pregnancy, and in the way of grand opera or stage tragedy, her young man left for the wars in Europe and was never heard of again.

In June 1802 Mary gave birth to a girl. There appears to be a strange aspect to the story of the birth, as recounted in the trial report, because it is stated there that Miss Surtees, the Colonel's daughter, called for a doctor on the day in which Mary went into labour. Somehow, for months, the pregnancy is supposed to have been concealed from the master's family. Poor Mary was warned of the dangers of 'destroying children' when in such a state of despair and disgrace. But the actual birth is the focus of attention for readers of the tale now, trying to understand what actually happened that Mary was charged with murder. It seems that she had a terrifyingly painful birth and, as the report at the time says:

> *Some time after, cries were heard . . . Half an hour after, blood was seen on the bed; and on search, a new-born female infant, dreadfully lacerated, was found between the bed and the mattress of an adjoining bed, its mouth was torn down to the throat, and its jawbone forced away.*

A Pontefract surgeon witnessed this and appeared in court to verify the medical condition of the child. He considered that there was some explanation, bearing in mind the girl's distraught state. Through modern eyes, we can see the potential delirium and even hallucination that attends on the stresses of birthing, but then it was almost impossible for temporary insanity to be ascertained and made to sound convincing in court. The surgeon simply stuck to his opinion and the lawyer prosecuting admitted that the case described was improbable but not impossible.

The jury, then, were being ask to consider the possibility that Mary had attacked the child in a fit of rage and despair, out of her wits, and then hidden the corpse. Her statement in explanation was that she never meant the baby any harm. She said: 'I cannot recollect how or where I did it; if I did, God knows. I loved my child before I saw it.' She said again: 'I am a wretched woman. It was my child; I never meant it any harm.'

Fittingly, even the judge, a man seasoned to face this kind of lamentable situation, gave the sentence with some expression of emotion, after Mary had been found guilty of wilful murder. A week later Mary Chapel was hanged at York, but to the very end she never expressed any feeling that she was guilty; she insisted that she must have done the deed in a fit of delirium. Poor Mary was so tough in her last moments that she even endured a wait as there was a problem with the knotting of the rope. The massive crowds who usually gathered on the Knavesmire for a show and entertainment were not in such a mood that day. They were subdued, and a report from the time says that Mary '. . . died without a struggle, amid the audible sobs of the multitude.'

What made the whole business so difficult in court was that Mary had evidently killed the baby with her own hands; there was no evidence of any weapon being used. As one writer twenty years after the event noted: 'Those who know the dreadful weakness attendant upon an accouchement, especially in the moment after the delivery, will see how impossible it is that she could have forced the jawbone away after the birth.' Either the child was killed in an agonising part of the birthing, or – and this is a long shot – some other person, wanting to help the girl in her desperate situation, did the killing for her.

CHAPTER 7

A Violent Temperament: Ann Haywood 1804

Her temper had, more than once, deprived her of her situations.

Ann Haywood was born in 1782, the daughter of ordinary working people. She had no proper education and it appears that there was no real moral guidance and parenting in her background. But, as with so many other girls, her destiny was to go into service. What was remarked, though, by commentators on this case, was that she had moods. She was apparently of a violent nature and it was noted that: 'Her temper had, more than once, deprived her of situations.'

This last statement implies that she drifted from job to job, losing her place and having to work hard to regain a good reputation. But all this comes to nothing in the face of what happened to her – a fate common to perhaps thousands of young women in this period, as we have seen with other infanticide cases. She was courted and then dropped and abandoned. In April 1804 she found that she was pregnant. The man who had fathered the child had said he intended marriage but then he backed out of that promise.

But there is no record of what might have followed, i.e. a suit for affiliation. Instead, she travelled on and went to work in Rotherham, for a family called Roodhouse. As with Mary Chapel, she somehow managed to hide the fact that she was with child and carried on her duties. Incredibly, she went on with her daily routine even to the point at which she was about to give birth. It seems hard to believe that this could be done, and it seems more likely that she had confided in a workmate and that there had been some help and support for her. The tale told at the time, before her trial, was that she came downstairs to work on 30 November and then began to go into labour. She went to a building outside the main home to have the child and another servant covered for her. This was surely the behaviour of a woman with amazing strength.

As with Mary Chapel, a similar situation then followed. She was alleged to have murdered the newborn child. The tale told in court was that she had returned to work, with smears of blood on her garments but had spun a story to cover and then carried on. If this had happened then she must have been in agony. Ann Haywood had supposedly stabbed the child many times and then stashed the body out of sight in the outhouse. We only have the minimal account of the family response after that; all that is known is that the mistress of the house knew that something was amiss with her young servant and had her sent away to Mosborough.

Not long after, as she was away from the home, the body of the child was found and the inevitable inquiry for the inquest began. As with Chapel, Ann denied the murder, and said that she had been in such a distressed condition that day that she had no real knowledge of her actions. It comes as no surprise to a modern reader to be told this.

At the Spring Azzises, Ann stood in the dock at York, facing a murder charge. She pleaded not guilty; it was obvious to writers at the time that she was still a sick woman. Mrs Roodhouse stated that Ann had been ill during that period up to the killing but that she had continued working. 'She complained much of cold in her limbs,' she said. Then the full story of the day of the birth emerged, after another servant testified that on that morning she had gone out to milk the cows, covering for Ann, who was staggering around in the kitchen. When they searched for her later, she was eventually found in the outhouse and, said the maid: 'Her hands were covered with blood.' Mrs Roodhouse took things in hand and made sure that Ann was washed and put to bed. Then a search began for the cause of the bloody state of the girl. A penknife was found first, under Ann's bed. It took another two days before the body of the baby was found. It was a little girl, the body covered in cuts and slashes.

A surgeon from Rotherham, Mr Wilkinson, testified that the corpse had two deep cuts on the face and a deep cut from the ear to the belly. The child was had been disembowled. He stated that the collar bone and ribs had been 'cut through'. Everything he said in terms of the physiology suggested the work of a small blade. Wilkinson also confirmed that when examined at that time, Ann was definitely in the condition of a recent parturition: 'The prisoner's appearance indicated a recent delivery' he found 'her breasts full and inflamed.'

Ann Haywood herself made a statement and this insisted that she knew nothing of the events leading up to the child's death: 'I might have borne the child in the outhouse, but I did not murder it.' She explained the state of the knife by saying that she had used it on a bird in doing some cooking that day. When she was pronounced guilty and sentenced to death she flung herself to the ground, begging for mercy. She listened to the terrible sentence with 'hysterical sobs'.

In the death cell, Ann confessed to the crime and in her desperation she repeatedly asked for the father of the child to be brought to her. Typical of those hard times, though, on the scaffold she had to share the last moments of her life with Wilkinson and they prayed together. As with the case of Chapel, the crowd was not as boisterous as usual and a writer noted that: 'The number of the females in the crowd was very great.' Ann faced her death with composure and courage. A reporter who saw her die noted that 'The drop fell and she expired without a struggle.'

Up to the time when many capital offences were taken from the statute books (in Prime Minister Peel's period of office in the 1830s), 359 people were sentenced to hang for murder between 1814 and 1834. Of these, 309 were actually hanged, so there were commutations to penal servitude. But it is shameful and disgusting to report that such commutations for infanticide were rare. A man who had shot a gamekeeper was more likely to have his neck saved than a poor distraught girl who was pregnant and abandoned to a life of disgrace and poverty.

CHAPTER 8

The Deadly Mary Bateman 1809

Her offences were seen as even more damnable when it was learned that she had attempted to practise witchcraft even while in prison ...

York Castle has a long and often grim, disturbing history, and some of the most remarkable tales in the history of crime are set in this formidable and dark place. Not all of these stories have the glamour and myth of Dick Turpin, but they do tell us a great deal about a turbulent period in English social history.

The York dungeons housed many criminals, many poor unfortunate wretches and some hardened killers during the years of English history when the number of capital offences was in three figures, and law and order were hard to find. But violence was rife in the early years of the nineteenth century, and highwaymen and footpads were everywhere, and riots were always likely to break out in the underclass. The Combination Acts of 1799 to 1800 showed the paranoia of the Government after seeing the terror of the French Revolution just across the Channel. These acts made it illegal for people to gather in small groups in the streets.

One of the most heinous crimes must be that of the young mother who murdered just to make her own way in life, and had even dabbled in black magic. At five o'clock on a chill Monday morning in March 1809, forty-one-year-old Mary Bateman was brought from her cell in York to keep her date with the hangman. Knowing that pregnant women were spared the noose, she had tried to 'plead her belly' to save her neck, but it was no use. A massive crowd gathered. They wanted their entertainment and to see justice done.

What had she done, this woman from Aisenby near Thirsk, to come to such a sorrowful end? The jury were in no doubt that she had poisoned Rebecca Perigo of Bramley, near Leeds. Her crime had been carried out in such a protracted and cunningly planned way that her evil was seen to be more outrageous and callous than many another poisoning case of the time. Mary had schemed to defraud Rebecca, and was clearly aiming to poison another victim who was suspecting her of the crime, when she was apprehended. When arrested, a phial of deadly poison was found on her. This had happened in 1806, when apparently Rebecca was suddenly ill with a seizure (a 'flacking' in the local dialect) and collapsed. It was generally held that some evil curse had been put on her. But Mary Bateman developed into a controlling force on the Perigos, and she sent them pudding and

Mary Bateman, from Thomas's York Castle. Author's collection

honey. These foods were to be the means of poisoning. The *Newgate Calendar* states that '. . . the most important testimony was that of Mr Chorley the surgeon, who distinctly proved that he had analysed what remained of the pudding and of the honey pot, and that he found them both to contain a deadly poison called corrosive spirit of mercury. . .'

If the cause of death was indeed mercury poisoning, then the stuff would have had to be well saturated in the food, because mercury gives off a very toxic vapour. The substance probably used here was mercuric chloride, a corrosive chemical which in an amount of fifteen grains would bring about heart failure, with horrible burning of the mouth and the stomach in the initial period after consumption.

Mary Bateman was said to have been a nasty piece of work from her youth. According to the *Newgate Calendar*: 'Within two months of her marriage she was found to have been guilty of many frauds'. That same source says that it was in 1799 that she moved to live in Marsh Lane, Leeds, to 'deal in fortune telling and the sale of charms'.

Her offences were seen as even more devious and damnable when it was learned that she had attempted to practise witchcraft, even while in prison. She had extorted money from a young girl who wanted to see her sweetheart, by sewing a charm and coins into her dress: a charm that would mysteriously force the young man she loved to come and visit her in the gaol. Naturally, when it didn't work, the material was torn open and the coins were gone – into Mary's pocket. There had been plenty of other 'cunning folk' around the Leeds area, and it is useful here to bear in mind just how popular they were, so we can understand Bateman's success. As Owen Davies, a specialist on this subject, has written:

> *Prior to the infamy generated by Bateman's trial, however, the most well-known practitioner in Leeds was a wise man known as Rough Robin. For much of his career he could be found in an isolated spot on Rombald's Moor . . . People travelled from across the Pennines to consult him . . .*

In that atmosphere, we can understand how Bateman duped her victims. But she was brought to the York Assizes and faced her fate.

At the trial, when Mary claimed she was pregnant, the scene almost dissolved from solemnity into farce. The judge wanted a group of matrons in the court to examine Mary to prove her condition and wisely, as no one wanted to be involved in this, the good ladies of York began to shuffle out of the courtroom with some indignation. But the law prevailed. The judge ordered the doors to be shut so that the women had no choice but to comply and Mary was duly inspected, pronounced not with child, and so the sentence was passed. The trial had lasted for eleven hours.

The gaoler, who was with her on her last night, noted that she wrote a letter to her husband and sent her wedding ring home to be given to her daughter. She had her youngest child in the cell with her, to suckle, and it was a scene that the Ordinary (the officer who normally interviewed and monitored statements by prisoners) noted with feelings of sympathy. However, he also remarked on her silence regarding the crimes she had committed – and felt sure that she knew much more about other suspicious deaths connected with her activities. In the end, these secrets went to the grave with her.

At this time, notable killers and footpads attracted great crowds at their executions, and Mary Bateman was no exception. Though there were no friends to swing on her legs and quicken her death, there was, nevertheless, a crowd to prove her status as a dubious celebrity. A massive crowd had travelled from Leeds, where she had murdered, to see justice done of course. The hanging took place at the new drop, behind the Castle. It was eerily quiet when Mary said a prayer, but a shudder went through the crowd when she begged for mercy and shouted that she was innocent.

Her body was taken away to be used for medical dissection, all the way to Leeds by hearse. But, as with all celebrities, her death provoked a general curiosity to view the body and Mary's was no exception. So many people came to look at her corpse that the money raised was £80 14s – a great deal of cash then. It was given to the General Infirmary. This was all due to the opportunism of the enterprising William Hey, who saw the chance for some easy fund-raising.

Mary Bateman was destined to be the subject of ballads, chapbooks and tales by the fireside for many years to come

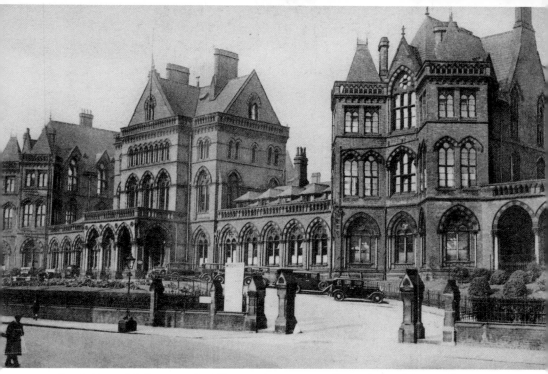

Leeds General Infirmary, where Bateman's corpse was dissected. Author's collection

throughout Yorkshire, in a time when killers and robbers attracted more attention that conventional heroes such as military men. She figured prominently in the *Newgate Calendar* in the 1820 period of its issue. It appears that she was full of tricks and cons, even on one occasion having a hen appear to lay an egg with 'Christ is Coming' written on the shell. So she became the stuff of myth and tall tales. After all, this was the time when 'Old Boney' (Napoleon Bonaparte) would come and get naughty children. Maybe others were threatened with a visit from the restless spirit of Mary the Poisoner?

One macabre coda to her story is that, as reported in *Yorkshire Notes and Queries* for 1891, the editor notes that 'The tongue of Mary Bateman is in the possession of a gentleman in Ilkley, with whom we are personally acquainted. There is absolutely no doubt as to its genuineness. The curious reader may see it at any time by the courtesy of the present owner.'

CHAPTER 9

The Killing of James Barber 1821

There had been some disturbance in the neighbourhood about a man called Thompson . . .

Ann (surname unknown) was born in 1784 into a poor family, and later, when her crime had entered the chronicles of Yorkshire murder, people pointed out that her parents were Ranters, a sect formed in 1648. This was a group which, according to the *Oxford Dictionary of British History*, 'scandalised the Godly by their unbridled dancing, drinking, smoking, swearing and sharing of sexual partners'. When she was twenty-one she married James Barber, a respectable man working as a general labourer. But the seeds of this murder were sown after several years of that marriage, when she met a man called Thompson, who lodged with them. When he came into their lives, they had been married for sixteen years and they had two children, one of fifteen and one of nine years old.

As with Elizabeth Broadingham, Barber left her husband to live with Thompson, moving with him to Potovens, but then returning home. They had been thrown out of that lodgings, near Wakefield, by John Holmes, who realised that they were not man and wife. She went home in January, and two months later her husband was dead. Unusually for the time and place, the surgeons called in to perform an autopsy on Barber's corpse were very thorough, in spite of the fact that one of them had no experience in that branch of medicine, and he made it clear to the court in York that he was a novice in those matters.

Barber had died of arsenic poisoning so Ann was the only suspect. An Oulton doctor, John Hindle, was the beginner in post-mortem work, and he had the thoroughness of the man who is learning his trade and going about it meticulously.

Ann Barber, from an old print. Clifford Elmer

The coroner's inquest was held at Barber's house and Hindle went to work. He found extensive evidence of poison in the corpse. He stated later in court that he had taken white arsenic from the coats of the stomach. He said: 'I know no other substance that would make the lungs so very black. I never saw anyone opened, but I have seen persons who have taken poison, and their external appearance agreed with Barber's.'

Here was a strange legal situation indeed: a learner surgeon taking long deliberation over his tentative inspections of a supposedly murdered man. But the case for the Crown was strengthened by the fact that another medical man worked with Hindle. The general view was that the victim must have 'taken more than a drachm', which would have been an eighth of an ounce. When cross-examined, Hindle confirmed that many of the external marks on the body would have been caused by convulsions. The defence tried to make the most of the surgeon's inexperience, asking whether or not he had done certain tests. But both Hindle and a surgeon from Rothwell, called Posketh, agreed that 'the lungs could not have been so black in so short a time unless mineral poison had been administered'.

Ann Barber had a motive, for sure. In the community it was said, with hindsight, that: 'There had been some disturbance in the neighbourhood about a man called Thompson.' That proved to be an extreme understatement, of course. A neighbour verified the state of the body just after death, as she was called to help lay out the corpse by Ann Barber's mother, Jane Smirthwaite. This woman, Sarah Parker, said that the man's ears had been black and that there had been a repulsive substance running from his mouth as they laid him out.

When Jane Smirthwaite gave evidence, she said that she had called the neighbour Sarah Parker on the evening before the

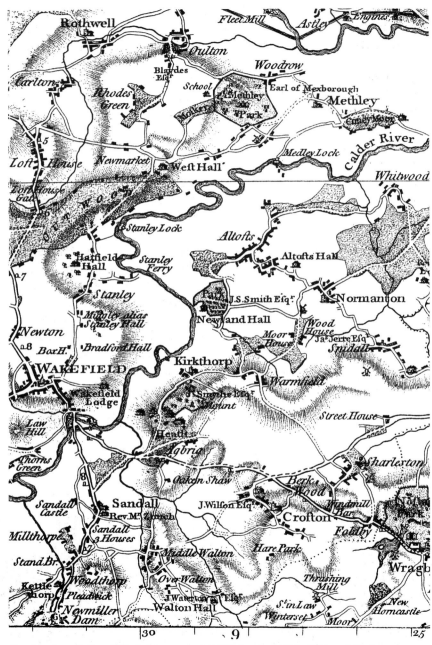

Extract from Jeffreys' Yorkshire map of 1775 showing Wakefield and Oulton. Author's collection

death, as James Barber had been saying that he was going to die. She said that she and Parker prayed with the dying man. But other details began to emerge at that point, such as the fact that Barber had fallen from a cart in the street. It seems that there had been trouble in the streets, some kind of public disorder, and he had been stressed and anxious about it all. The court must have been waiting to hear a full account of what had actually happened on the last night of Barber's life, and at last those details came when a certain Thomas Spurr gave evidence. Spurr lived fairly close at Rhodes Green. He and Barber's brother had been with James Barber on the final night, and Spurr said that he told Ann that she had 'a physician for the soul and you want a physician for the body as well as the soul'. It seems highly likely, from the latter's statement and the worries about noise and violence in the streets outside, that Barber's 'soul' was in trouble. Spurr, though, before leaving, had not thought Barber to be a dying man. It is also clear that Thompson had become the victim of what is often called 'rough music' in the community, harassed and booed for taking a man's wife from him. Paradoxically, Barber himself had received similar taunting, as one witness said that one evening there had been a row at the Barbers' door and the neighbours had been yelling out that the man was a cuckold.

Cottages at Oulton, from a Victorian magazine. Author's collection

Clearer evidence of Ann Barber's actions came from a son of a constable, who gave information about Ann's purchase of mercury. She had bought a pennyworth at Wakefield from a druggist called Reinhardt. She had told the constable that after buying the poison she had put some in some warm ale and sugar given to her husband. Her motive was that she was 'stalled of him.' The prosecution therefore ended with a statement about an alleged confession, and some details of Barber being seen looking in the window of Reinhardt's druggist's.

Vaguely, as a flimsy defence made of a few random bits of hearsay, there was recorded anecdotal evidence that Barber had threatened to do away with himself. That was patently absurd, and if he had chosen mercury or arsenic as his exit from the world, then it made no sense. There were other less painful ways to die. Equally, if there was no definite evidence that Ann had bought the poison in Wakefield, there were strong hints that she had, and no evidence to the contrary.

This mess was resolved when the judge clarified the issues. The central issue was that if Ann Barber did administer the poison, with intent to kill her husband, then the crime was petty treason. The jury, if in doubt, could decide instead on murder. But the jury infact stated: 'She is guilty of petty treason and murder.' It must have appeared as if they wanted their pound of flesh. After all, there was no real defence and no other suspect. The autopsy made foul play a certainty.

The judge said directly to Ann: 'As far as my understanding can judge, no reasonable creature can have any doubt about your guilt.' Basically, Ann refuted the point that she had ever been in the druggist's shop, but it did her no good. She was sentenced to death and as a matter of course she was given the chance to 'plead her belly' if she was pregnant. But that was not the case. To the scaffold she went, a week later, and a witness noted that 'there was nothing interesting in her countenance', as if he had expected something dramatic from her. One detail is important: her crime was petty treason, and she would have been normally dragged on a cart through the mob to the scaffold, but this was not done. The witness said, plainly: 'She received spiritual consolation and died without a struggle.' One loose end, picked up by writer Rede Leman, was the involvement of the shadowy Thompson. Leman wrote: 'Why was there

no implication upon Thompson, the tendency might have
further elucidated this dreadful case?' We also have to ask if
there was a possibility that Barber was in fact driven to suicide,
where was the help for him when he was being victimised and
bullied for his weakness in allowing the adultery to continue?
The Barber case is indeed, by any standards, a dreadful case,
with a puzzle at the centre and very shoddy work performed in
the court by the professionals at the time.

CHAPTER 10

Ursula Lofthouse: Hanged with Two Men 1835

She was the last victim of Curry, the bungling hangman . . .

This is a harrowing story, and yet in some ways it is more the narrative of the hangman than the hanged. Ursula Lofthouse was the last woman to be publicly hanged in Yorkshire, and the hangman was John Curry, a man with a drink problem. Of all the professions in the world, the one of hangman is surely the one in which we expect the trade being done to be done soberly. Ursula Lofthouse was hanged along with two men, on 6 April 1835, for poisoning her husband. But her murder was ordinary fare compared with the actions of Curry.

The record will go down with the horrific statement: 'She was the last victim of Curry the bungling hangman.' Over a period of thirty-three years, Curry did around 117 executions. He had been a convicted felon himself (that was the usual practice in the years before the profession was more regulated). What perhaps tells us most about the man is the tale of his work in 1821, when he was to hang two men, starting with highwayman Michael Shaw. He had to pass several public houses in York as he made his way to the second appointment, where the thief William Brown was waiting for him.

Curry was the worse for drink when he arrived, and on the scaffold he swung the rope in the air and challenged the restless crowd with the words: 'Some of you come up and try it!'. The report at the time stated:

The executioner, in a bungling manner and with great difficulty . . . placed the cap over the culprit's face and attempted several

A Victorian image of a woman being hanged. Illustrated Police News

times to place the rope round the neck but was unable. He missed the unfortunate man's head with the noose every time that he tried.

Ursula spent her last hours in the female prison (now incorporated into the Castle House Museum) and she was to hang at the 'new drop', not out on the Knavesmire where Dick Turpin had been hanged a century before. She was reported to have behaved stoically and it was recorded that she had got back at a man who had been physically violent to her – a common pattern in the days when, after all, women were often seen as property. In fact, only two years after Ursula Lofthouse's death, a man was to sell his wife. One Joshua Jackson was convicted of selling his wife, and given one month in prison.

As for Mr Curry, on Ursula's last day, he was amazingly in control, as was his charge. The male killers died first, and she had to watch them with the terrible knowledge of her forthcoming fate. They had killed in the course of a violent robbery; she had merely hit back, turned and acted after long abuse. Through modern eyes, there is no parity to be seen there. The moralists writing at the time had a lot to say about that, and it appears that Ursula's case had some impact on the general opinion of hanging women. Horrifically, another forty-nine female executions were to follow as public spectacles for the masses, the last in this category being Frances Kidder in Maidstone, on 2 April 1868. It is a stunning thought, to reflect that the old drunkard retired that April day, no doubt making his way to the nearest hostelry, whereas Ursula's body hung for some time, until she was cut down and her corpse taken to Leeds Infirmary to provide the medical students with some anatomical study. Up until 1833, women were hanged for offences other than murder, notably 'uttering' – forgery. The fact that hangings were public was a scandal, though both Charles Dickens and Thomas Hardy had a strange interest in seeing women hang. Ursula Lofthouse had to tolerate a crowd of about 2,000 when she left this life.

CHAPTER 11

Child Murders in Tough Victorian Towns

Mary drowned herself and her two children ... in a mill dam ...

In Bradford, in 1862, we have arguably the saddest and most poignant example of the kind of infanticide recorded all too often in the overcrowded, over-charged townships of the Industrial Revolution in Yorkshire. This is the story of Mary Ryan, a wife who was beaten and kicked by her idle husband, victimised to such a degree that one day she walked out of the basement with her two children and walked to her death, taking the children with her to eternity. Mary drowned herself and her two children (the youngest only nine months old) in a mill dam in Frederick Street.

The Victorian press gives us all too common evidence of such desperate acts, by women at the edge of reason. Mary Ryan's story is a reminder of what Hardy fictionalised in the tale of the suicide and child murder in *Jude the Obscure*: sheer end-of-tether death when life is perceived as being without value to anyone. But at the other end of the spectrum, there is the child murder that is done by a woman in such a crazed state that it has Gothic horror in its narrative. Such was the case of Jane Crompton in Hull in May 1873. Crompton not only decapitated her child, but asked a neighbour in to witness the killing happen. A mark of Crompton's insanity is in her answer to a question about why she had done such a dreadful thing. She replied that she would not have done so 'if the neighbours had treated me properly'. One would have thought, as historian Steve Jones has written, that this was a case for 'care rather than punishment' but in fact she was indicted for murder.

A horrendous case took place in Howarth, and the man in question was John Sagar, master of the workhouse at Oakworth. A memorial stone in Haworth's churchyard commemorates the

Bradford centre around 1920. Author's collection

deaths of nine children and also their mother, Barbara. It is almost certain that John poisoned them. So in this case the killer was a man, but in virtually all child murders the poor distraught woman perpetrator was left with no choice, or was without rational control of her mind at the time.

As Clive Emsley has pointed out: 'Until 1803 the crime of infanticide was supposed to be tried under an act of 1624 which defined the offence as one committed specifically by an un-married woman.' But of course this was not maintained in its severity as time went on. Gradually, as the nineteenth century progressed, some increased understanding of puerperal insanity and depression related to childbirth gradually emerged. The change may be observed in the case of Eliza Higgins in 1857, who was tried for murder of her daughter at the Old Bailey, but was convicted of manslaughter as an act of mercy. By 1866 one lawyer observed that there was 'a great reluctance to hang women'.

But in the northern towns this state of affairs took rather longer to happen. At the heart of the issue was the crucially im-portant need for a young woman to keep her good name, her position in society and her self-respect. This, naturally, had another undesirable side effect: at times the affiliation orders

THE PARSONAGE DOORWAY, HAWORTH. 7001

The more pleasant side of Howarth: the Brontë vicarage. Author's collection

after a bastard birth, demanding finance from putative fathers, meant that these men would sometimes run from the constraints and responsibilities, but would also be liable to encourage disposal of the child – surely a move seen as the easiest way out of all perceived problems. Under laws of 1733 and 1809, the unmarried mother simply had to name the supposed father and then the parish poor law overseers would move in. This fear was surely an inducement to find that murderous route out of problems. In 1852, for instance, Alfred Waddington of Sheffield killed his little daughter. He had been affiliated and 'he was ordered to pay two shillings a week for its support' but the *Annual Register* reported that: 'The prisoner was in arrears in his payments for the support of the child and a summons was issued against him ...' He killed the child with a shoemaker's knife.

There was nothing new in all this: it is simply that longstanding problems were exacerbated by the new industrial conditions and urban growth. Children had always been either killed or abandoned and left to the parish. In 1638, for instance, a certain Ursula Harcourt of Carleton, as was reported in the Quarter Sessions Records for the West Riding, ' ... is lately gone out of the country ... and hath left behind her children which are already chargeable'. The churchwardens and overseers of the poor were left to sort it out.

The period in which there was the highest incidence of infanticide was the 1850s and 1860s. As Josephine McDonagh has put it, at that time: 'Britain was stricken by an apparent epidemic of child murder.' A contemporary writer called Henry Humble, writing in 1866 about the epidemic, expressed the nature of the problem like this: 'Bundles are left lying about the streets, which people will not touch, lest the too familiar object – a dead body – should be revealed, perchance with a pitch plaster over its mouth or a woman's garter around its mouth.'

One typical example from Yorkshire happened at a railway station. In Wakefield, a baby was born to one Annie Scruton, and she paid Mary Robson (of Bridlington) to adopt the child. The latter was one of a class of baby-farmers and she collected the baby, then waited for a train at Normanton. The problem was that the child was sick. In the early hours, the baby was dead, lying on a bench in the waiting room. At the inquest, as

COMMITTEE ON INSANITY AND CRIME.

REPORT

OF THE

Committee appointed to consider what changes, if any, are
desirable in the existing law, practice and procedure
relating to criminal trials in which the plea of insanity
as a defence is raised, and whether any and, if so,
what changes should be made in the existing
law and practice in respect of cases falling
within the provisions of section 2 (4)
of the Criminal Lunatics Act, 1884.

Presented to Parliament by Command of His Majesty.

LONDON:
PRINTED & PUBLISHED BY HIS MAJESTY'S STATIONERY OFFICE.
To be purchased directly from H.M. STATIONERY OFFICE at the following addresses:
Imperial House, Kingsway, London, W.C.2; 28, Abingdon Street, London, S.W.1;
York Street, Manchester; 1, St. Andrew's Crescent, Cardiff;
or 120, George Street, Edinburgh;
or through any Bookseller.

1924

Price 8d. net.

Cmd. 2005.

Report on Insanity and Crime, 1924. Author's collection

with so many of these sad cases, the blame was difficult to apportion. The result was that there was a verdict of neglect – not manslaughter, which would have been quite likely had there been a culprit to point at. This kind of infanticide happened everywhere, and there was very little in place in terms of social support for the mothers who could not cope with the expense of having a child to care for.

It was a Yorkshire-based doctor, Edmund Syson, who told the Parliamentary Select Committee looking into the problem, that earlier in his career when he was a doctor near Rotherham, he had found out just how open a topic this was: 'I have been asked myself to kill a child as it was being born, and by a good-natured nurse too, and I'm sure she had no idea it was murder.' The historian Lionel Rose has explained the various methods used to 'kill off' unwanted babies. Obviously suffocation ('lying on') was common, but also the vital organs could be punctured with needles, injuries to the head and neck could be put down to a difficult delivery and, at times, a bucket was used so that the child could be drowned as soon as it emerged from the mother's body.

Finally, reference should be made in this survey to one of the most unusual and brutal substances used to murder a new-born child. This was the case of Ann Hinchcliffe of Knottingley who, in 1867, used creosote to end the life of her daughter's unwanted child. Amazingly, though statements had been made about creosote being purchased from a shop run by a Mr Garforth, Hinchcliffe was acquitted. She had sent her own grandson several bottles of the stuff over a period, and the family knew that the woman had referred to the child as 'an encumbrance', and yet she escaped the law.

As time went on, Victorian society began to understand the pressures on single women in this context of moral condemnation and dire economic necessity. George Eliot, the novelist, played her part: in her novel *Adam Bede* (1859), the main female character Hetty Sorel is seduced into 'infamy' and Eliot makes it clear that Hetty could not possibly have supported a child. Serious literary treatment of the subject was needed to counteract the depiction of female killers in the popular press and the broadsheets, which gathered all the details they could

ADAM BEDE

BY

GEORGE ELIOT

AUTHOR OF

"SCENES OF CLERICAL LIFE"

"So that ye may have
Clear images before your gladden'd eyes
Of nature's unambitious underwood
And flowers that prosper in the shade. And when
I speak of such among the flock as swerved
Or fell, those only shall be singled out
Upon whose lapse, or error, something more
Than brotherly forgiveness may attend."

WORDSWORTH.

IN THREE VOLUMES

VOL I.

WILLIAM BLACKWOOD AND SONS
EDINBURGH AND LONDON
MDCCCLIX

The Right of Translation is reserved.

Title page to Eliot's Adam Bede, *1859.* Author's collection

find of a woman criminal's 'deviance' from the norms of accept-able womanhood.

As an actual classified crime, infanticide did not exist until 1922. In the seventeen years before the Infanticide Act of that year, sixty women had been given the death sentence for killing their newborn children, but all were reprieved except one. Appeals to the Home Secretary on that issue were generally suc-cessful for obvious reasons. By that statute, killing a child was reduced from murder to manslaughter in that near-birth con-text. In the Act it states:

> *Where a woman, by any wilful act or omission, causes the death of her newly-born child, but from the time had not fully recovered from the effect of giving birth to such child, and by reason thereof the balance of her mind was disturbed, then she shall be guilty of infanticide.*

On the other hand, in 1929 the Infant Life (Preservation) Act tackled the question of a person killing before birth, wording carefully the proviso that the exception to manslaughter here would be 'an act done in good faith to preserve the life of the mother.' Even today, the issue is alive and problematical, but we do have more advanced medical science and we have statistics. Perhaps the most telling of these facts is to informa-tion that around 2 per cent of mothers now (10,000 women a year) suffer from post-natal traumatic stress disorder. We have to wonder how many of those women in the northern industrial towns had that illness and paid for the irrational killings they committed with their lives.

There is also the question of inevitable poverty that lay beneath this crime in the Victorian period. *The Parliamentary Papers* for 1843 talk about 'a girl's road to ruin' and the slip from poverty to prostitution is explained like this:

> *Suppose the poor creature* [in a mill or factory] *be put on half time, or to be thrown out of work altogether, she has no parents, no friends to fall back on, resources she has none, what then is the alternative? The answer is obvious.*

Through the long melancholy history of child murder in our society, instances in which women have escaped the noose, in the years up to the mid-nineteenth century, are rare. The

Perhaps the most famous victim of the pillory: Titus Oates, from an old print.
Author's collection

example in Long Riston, near Beverley, for instance, in 1799, was unusual. The woman was pilloried and then transported. This is strange indeed. In Beverley, the pillory had not been there long. In 1783 the Beverley Corporation Minute Book records that: 'A temporary pillory to be made and Ald. Middleton to make the same.' There had been a pillory centuries before, and it was usually butchers who had sold bad meat who

A whipping-post, from a Victorian magazine. Author's collection

were subjected to that humiliation. It is terrible to contemplate the woman in question, in that last year of the eighteenth century (when the supposed Age of Reason was in existence, we read), as she stood in the pillory, with the knowledge that the locals knew exactly what she had done.

CHAPTER 12

Alice Levick
1854

A man had come behind her and murdered the child ...

Some killings (or possible ones) have of course been committed by Yorkshire people just over the border, as it were. In this case it is in Warwickshire – the northern part of that county being a place where men were recruited from fieldwork to go and work in south Leeds and in the south Yorkshire coalfields. In the late nineteenth century there was a regular flow of labour from villages such as Bulkington to Yorkshire, and one such link provides the basis for this terrible story. A young girl from a Yorkshire branch of a family called Downey went to see her aunt and all kinds of mayhem broke out.

It is a remarkable story of a terrible killing done by a Yorkshire female, Alice Levick – of only ten years old. It took place at Brandon in Warwickshire, where the girl had gone to live, and before her had come information of her good character, and she was taken in by a family, as a poor orphan from South Yorkshire, just a few miles away. But the Downey family were in for a shock when this seemingly sweet young girl came among them. She had what we would now recognise as profound psychological problems.

James Beech was a gamekeeper in the area, and his little son, Francis was just ten years old when Alice Levick arrived. Along with James was Donald Downey, also a gamekeeper. The girl was the niece of Mrs Downey and had only been there for around three weeks when it became clear that she liked to go her own way. She was headstrong and had a penchant for leaving home and wandering wherever she fancied. Mrs Downey remonstrated with her for this. But the girl was useful as well, running errands and generally earning her keep.

One day Mrs Downey sent the girl to collect some cutlery which had been borrowed by some charcoal burners, and Alice took little Francis with her. So began a mysterious series of events out in the woods. The charcoal burners, John Nicks and John Brooks, while working became aware of someone shouting. One of them heard a child crying out 'Oh dear!' and eventually people went to see what was happening, but soon, out into the clearing came Alice, carrying the baby. A contemporary report describes the scene in this way:

> *When they got up to her she told them that a man had come softly behind her then tied a handkerchief over her face, and then murdered the child. On taking the child from her they found that it was quite dead and cold.*

The girl told her story again but it was becoming increasingly muddled and garbled. At first she said that she had been blindfolded, then she said it might have been a man or a woman who did the deed. She said that she panicked when she heard a hooting noise, but then took the baby up from the ground and ran homewards as fast as she could.

What had really happened out there in the woods? Found at the scene of the crime was a piece of brown paper on the grass with knives and forks lying on it. One knife was lying separate from the rest and there was also a white handkerchief soaked in blood. One of the witnesses to the child's tale at the time said simply: 'A man had come behind her and murdered the child.' Some tried to think whether the gamekeeper had enemies who might have done this, as his occupation was one that tended to create vendettas and long-standing hatred from the poaching community. The field where it happened was called Van Dieman's Land locally, surely a name suggestive of that ancient history of enmity between keepers and poachers. The girl had apparently said that a man came up to her and said: 'Little girl, leave me the knives and the baby . . .'. A local police officer testified that she had said this to him.

As for the girl, she was a loner and would have been the type to live in a world of play and make-believe. Making up a story would not have been hard for her, some said.

She had told a weird and wonderful tale, one that nobody believed. Medical opinion in the case generally agreed that her account did not accord with the circumstances at the scene or with child's wounds, but one surgeon pointed out that there was a large wound on the side of the child's neck in keeping with the use of a knife such as the one found at the scene. But surely a young girl could not have used that weapon with such force. The girl's clothes had been in disarray, so it was not impossible that she had been involved in some kind of struggle, but the conclusion was that she was probably guilty of the killing. She was duly charged but in court the jury found her not guilty of wilful murder. Mr Spooner, for the defence, begged the jury to 'give credence to the girl'.

Beneath the slender layer of facts and details of the scene there surely lie two other stories, one being something maybe akin to the fantasy and bizarre personal imagination we find in more recent child killers such as Mary Bell in Newcastle: some kind of enactment of fantastic childish indulgence that led to this horrendous death. But the other theme is arguably a tale of a local poacher out for revenge, who took his chance to settle a grudge in Van Dieman's Land field.

CHAPTER 13

Charlotte Barton:
The Hammer Murder
1870

I have hit Padgin with a hammer ...

In the Victorian period, a high proportion of people cohabited, especially in the industrial towns, where strict moral rectitude was perhaps less of a problem for couples with regard to the immediate neighbours. It often made practical sense to have a younger woman 'living in' and being basically a mix of wife and 'domestic'. The story of Charlotte Barton, however, highlights some of the problems with these arrangements when things go wrong.

Thomas Padgin was fifty-seven and he worked as a shoemaker. Before the fateful events of December 1870, he and Charlotte had lived together reasonably happily for twelve years. The *Police News* report says that they were known as 'quiet people' and that Charlotte kept a respectable house, taking pride in her housework. Padgin was described as 'elderly' in the report, but that was perhaps partly related to the life expectancy of the time, and partly to the fact that he was ill. Although in his youth he had been sturdy and well, for some years before these events, he had suffered from a paralysis. He was unable to hold down a job and luckily he had finance coming to him from friendly societies and welfare clubs. But it does seem, reading between the lines of this horrible tale, that he was short of cash.

On Tuesday 8 December 1870, Charlotte snapped. She set about her partner with an intent to kill him, and the poor police constable who was sent to the house would have cast his eyes on very little that was unusual until he reached the steps leading down to the cellar. There, lying across some steps, was the body of Padgin, bent double, with his head pointing down the stairs. His corpse was mutilated, and it was later found that in no fewer than seven places there were severe injuries which had caused broken limbs or joints. It was a scene of carnage. A pool of blood had gathered at the foot of the stairs and in a little sink there was more blood. The *Police News* report including the following:

> *The body was removed to the upstairs room and laid on a couch. One eye was upturned, the other closed up, and shockingly bruised. The face on both sides was pounded into a mass of pulp and the head was dreadfully mangled.*

Why this had happened is a complex question, though Charlotte's explanation to her brother when she went to see him after the killing was straightforward enough. She said: 'He wanted me to go with other men.' The fact that she made strenuous efforts to clean up after the crazed attack suggests a deeply troubled mind. She apparently scrubbed clean most of the surfaces that had been spattered with blood, and she had tried to remove stains from the walls, though without real success.

In court, at the inquest, the killer gave some surprising facts or perhaps half-truths. She said that her husband was still living nearby, at Broad Lane, and that she had in fact married Padgin. But her mind was disintegrating, because when she was quizzed about this apparent bigamy, being asked if she had two husbands living she said, 'No, only one.'

The facts of the attack she had erased from her mind, and at the trial in Leeds, she denied using the axe in the attack. Wilful murder was the charge, and a crowd of friends and relatives appeared and showed much concern. The case was reported as being a tale of 'an unfortunate women' not a crazy axe-murderer, and so it seems. The sentence was the humane one: that Charlotte Barton was a lunatic, and was therefore unfit to plead. It was a sad case of incarceration in an asylum. It appears that the reality of what was happening to her never really sank in, as she kept a 'cool and indifferent demeanour' throughout the inquest and the trial itself.

Beneath the horrible bare facts of this murder there perhaps lies another story, something bound up inextricably with the couple's changing relationship under duress as the financial hardships set in, and the hint about her being asked to earn money by prostitution, however bizarre and deranged that might have seemed when stated, could well have a kernel of truth. It would have been the kind of pressure put upon a woman in those hard times well before the welfare state and at a time when the fear of the ultimate fall – the workhouse – was for many a genuine terror to be avoided at all costs.

When the woman walked to her brother's shop and said simply, 'I have hit Padgin with a hammer', this was surely a terrifyingly downbeat statement, as if talking into a mirror, expressing a piece of reality that was too hard to bear.

CHAPTER 14

'Never Wed an Old Man': Kate Dover
1881

... only a fine line divided the case from one of wilful murder.

The great judge Sir Henry Hawkins writes in his memoirs of a visit to Sheffield around the 1870s. He says that a colleague in that city said to him: 'The fumes from the factories Mr Hawkins, have so played the devil with our trees that the general impoverishment of nature has earned for the locality of Sheffield the unpleasant title of the Suburbs of Hell.' But in the mid-Victorian years it was not fumes but the people who created that hell. At the centre of much of this antagonism was the presence of poison, and this case is one of the most prominent from that time.

In some ways, this is a story of two women and a man, but not in the usual sense of a 'love triangle' or any similar situation involving jealousy or rancour. At the heart of it is a terrible death by arsenic poisoning, and an apparent killer who, at least on the surface, had no real motive for taking the victim's life.

In 1880 Kate Dover kept a small shop on London Road in Sheffield; she was a go-ahead fashion conscious young woman, twenty-eight years old and known to the locals as the 'Queen of Heeley'. It seems entirely in keeping that Kate would have been attracted to the personality and lifestyle of a local artist, Thomas Skinner, who lived in Lowfields. There was something about Kate that was stimulated by a bohemian attitude to life; the creativity in her was expressed in her appearance and in her ambitions. When she met Skinner, although he was over twenty years older than her, there was a rapport. He was held in high esteem by the town's artistic community, having thought up a

London Road, Sheffield, where Kate's shop was located. Laura Carter

new method of etching images on steel. This would be not only an artistic success, but one with commercial potential.

Kate and the older man became close, and she moved in as his housekeeper in the summer of 1880. So close were the two of them that Mrs Jones, the other domestic servant in the picture, left in high dudgeon. From that point on, Skinner and Kate enjoyed a good life together. But there is certain to be some causes of frustration when two such people live together – both creative and both vain to a high degree. When money was not quite in its usual easy supply for Kate's habits, disagreements happened. Their relationship was stormy; at one time Skinner would be furious with her (he once thought she had pawned some of his belongings – to feed her shopping habits), but there was plenty of evidence to suggest that they were emotionally close and dedicated to each other's happiness.

Marriage came onto the agenda, and Kate had said to a friend who had questioned the wisdom of that idea (perhaps bearing in mind the old song, *Maids when you're Young Never Wed an Old Man*), that she would rather be an old man's darling than a young man's slave. This was at the beginning of December

1881, and around that time the couple were in society and talking with others, so much so that someone would later recall that Skinner had been talking about buying Kate a pony. That had been just the day before the artist was to die in agony.

The familiar scenario of the woman of the house sending out for poison now enters the tale. Kate had sent a girl to buy chloroform first, and laudanum. There was nothing sinister in that, as both substances were in general use at the time for all kinds of maladies. But the staff at Learoyd's druggists wanted some assurance, and there is surely a sinister logic to the fact that following that attempt, Kate then went personally to another shop to buy two pennyworth of arsenic, ostensibly to 'colour some artificial flowers'. By this time, late in the century, the Arsenic Act of 1851 and further controls on retailing, had had some effect on what had formerly been an easy source of the means to murder someone, usually the spouse. But Kate, on being asked to return with a witness, did so with no problem, finding a man called Wood to sign and witness the purchase.

Then came the usual scene of a meal being cooked, and then the couple sitting down to eat. What we know from later information is that Kate cooked the fowl and some stuffing separately and when they began eating the fowl which was the main part of the meal, both were ill. But crucially, whereas Kate was merely vomiting the food back up, Skinner was in a far more serious state of pain and suffering. A doctor was called and he

Kate Dover's home in Sheffield. Laura Carter

Old Waggon and Horses, Heeley, Sheffield, where inquests were held. Author's collection

saw immediately that the man was in the throes of arsenic poisoning. By mid-evening that same day, Skinner was dead.

Dr Harrison, who lived in Cemetery Road, was efficient and sensible in everything he did at the scene of death, gathering the food that both people had eaten as samples for later study. He also noticed that Kate had burnt a document looking like a will. But Kate later said that Skinner had directed her to do that upon his death.

There was an inquest at the *Royal Hotel* on Abbeydale Road and this followed hard on a thorough post-mortem which had confirmed that the deceased had died from arsenical poisoning. Just before Christmas the inquest met again, and this time with fuller information about the condition of the corpse. The vital detail here was that there was no arsenic found in the stuffing – the food vomited up by Kate Dover. Mrs Jones made a statement and it was becoming clear that she deeply resented Kate's taking over at Skinner's house. Mention was then made of some love letters – and these involved another man in Kate's life. The pieces of a murderous situation were being placed, as in a jigsaw, and as the pieces were collected, the finger of guilt was pointing clearly at the young Queen of Heeley.

But things were not so simple, because the motive did not seem to be there. When Mr Wightman, the coroner, instructed the jury about potential verdicts, not all around the notional incidence of a homicide because it could have been an accidental death, the word 'murder' was in his vocabulary. When Kate then appeared in the dock at the magistrates' court, it was certain that it would have to go further and that Kate was to be charged. That was on Christmas Eve. The law took no time off. At Leeds Assizes in February 1882, she was on trial for her life. The circumstantial evidence directed thoughts towards her murderous intent, but it was more complex than that, as her defence lawyer, Frank Lockwood, made clear.

The trial was a major event for the general populace. A report in the *Sheffield & Rotherham Independent* notes that 'there was a great hustling outside the court, then pell mell, like a lot of schoolboys ... the ladies stormed the galleries ...'.

The central paradox for the jury was that though Kate had not eaten the same poisonous food as the dead man, and therefore appeared guilty of administering the arsenic, she was palpably happy with him and they had been seen just the previous night, content and at ease in each other's company. They were to marry, as well, so that seemed to cancel out any motive. Yet there was the matter of Kate's love letters, creating a suspicion of duplicity, planted in the minds of the jury and the public by the lurid reports of this in the local press.

The decisive factor was arguably in Lockwood's impassioned speech in which he said, 'the prisoner had everything to gain by the prolongation of life of the deceased ... and no living man or woman had seen the act committed'. He even managed to play down the purchase of the arsenic, saying that this was done '... in a perfectly straightforward manner and no attempt was made in any way to conceal her name, which she gave in full'.

The celebrated judge, a fellow of Lincoln College, Sir Lewis Cave, was not impressed by what appeared to be the gullibility of the jury in returning a verdict of manslaughter. He said that the jury had taken a 'merciful view of the case'. But he felt he had to say that 'only a fine line divided the case from one of wilful murder'. The humane alternative to the scaffold at that time was penal servitude for life. This was harsh within the guidelines of the sentencing tariffs set down in the Penal

The area where Kate's victim lived. Laura Carter

Servitude Acts of 1853 and 1854, which gave the judge the choice of any period over three years. Cave clearly thought Kate Dover was a murderess. Kate collapsed on hearing this sentence and she had to be carried down to the court cell.

A poem published in *Punch* just a few years later describes this scene well:

A terrible silence then reigned in the court,
and the eyes of humanity turned to the dock;
her head was bent down and her sobbing came short,
and the jailer stood ready with hand on the lock
of the gate of despair, that would open no more
when this wreckage of beauty was hurried away . . .

CHAPTER 15

The Wombwell Murderers 1903

Give it to him Johnny, punch him to death!

In John Ellis's memoirs, *Diary of a Hangman*, he included a chapter called 'How I Hanged a Woman.' Here, he compares the case of Edith Thompson to that of Barnsley killer Emily Swann:

> *Twice before I had been concerned with the execution of a woman. The first was in 1903, when I was assistant hangman at the double execution of John Gallagher and Emily Swann, at Armley Gaol, Leeds, for the brutal murder of Mrs Swann's husband. The other was twenty years later when Mrs Sarah Newell paid the penalty in Duke Street prison, Glasgow, for killing a 12-year-old newsboy . . . Both these women were coarse and rather vulgar, very different from Edith Thompson.*

Ellis had been appointed as an assistant in 1901 and was tutored by the notorious William Billington. He had a tough initiation but it is interesting that he makes no more mention of Emily Swann, despite the fact that he was only learning the trade and was clearly very nervous when he had to watch Billington hang Swann and Gallagher just after Christmas in 1903. Instead, he chooses to focus on an execution in Newcastle involving a young murderer called Miller. When he does choose to write about the horrendous experience of hanging a woman, at the beginning of his book (where he wants the maximum impact), he chooses Thompson, someone more overtly representative of 'feminine' character and lifestyle.

All this tells us a great deal about Emily Swann. Ellis returns to the case later in his book, and his account of the crime, the woman's character and her dying is heart-rending. Her story is

John Ellis, the hangman. Laura Carter

easily reduced to elemental and basic emotional forces: a small woman who was physically abused by her husband who then takes a lover and finds happiness, but the violence of her husband continues. Such a tale is bound to end in confrontation and a retribution, and so indeed it was.

But this paragraph only gives the essence, almost like a folk tale. What we need to do to understand the case is to start with the Swanns themselves. They lived in George Square, Wombwell, and they were in the habit of taking in lodgers. When John Gallagher arrived, he and Emily soon became fond of each other and an affair began. When William Swan found out he reacted by throwing Gallagher out. But the lovers continued to see each other. On 5 June 1903, Gallagher had come back to visit Emily, so obviously there was friction, and Swann was his usual truculent self. Gallagher, small though he was, made it clear that if Swann harmed Emily again, he would come looking for him.

That happened sooner than any of them must have thought. In fact the very next day the lovers met in the home of a Mrs Ward and after they had talked a while, Emily went home. But soon she was back, and the first act of the tragedy was to begin. She was badly busied and had black eyes. As soon as she said, 'See what our Bill has done!' it was the trigger for Gallagher to act. He left, swearing to punish the husband for what he had done.

From that point things got out of hand. Though Gallagher was only slight and lightly built he was handy with his fists and a titanic struggle followed in the Swann house. The fight was so loud and public that neighbours heard and saw things that would later be very important evidence. The most striking statement overheard was Emily shouting: 'Give it to him Johnny, punch him to death!'

When the first confrontation had petered out, Gallagher returned to Mrs Ward's house and started to say that he had broken some of Swann's ribs. He said that he would 'go and give him something for himself for that'. This kind of aggression had been going on for some time, and this day was going to be the end of it. Gallagher said that he had 'busted four ribs and that he would go bust some more'. There were a number of witnesses, naturally, to all this trouble.

For a while since leaving the Swanns, Gallagher had been planning to go to Bradford, and on this day was heard to say in Mrs Ward's home: 'I'll finish him off before I go to Bradford.' There was a clear intention to kill in that statement, and he also was heard to say: 'I'll murder the pig before morning. If he can't kick a man he shan't kick a woman!' The fight went on in George Square and again Emily's voice was heard saying: 'Give it to him Johnny.'

The end of this battle indoors was that the lovers emerged from her home, hand in hand, and a bystander said that they stood 'with every sign of affection'. There had been over ten minutes of fighting and screaming. Over the years, Emily had often been beaten by her husband, and that moment when she and her lover came out of the door was surely a moment of freedom for her, whatever the circumstances. The circumstances were that in the house behind them, William Swann lay dead.

It didn't take long for the police to be called and to be on their way, but Gallagher escaped and took to the open road, leaving Emily to face the music. She was arrested but Gallagher was on the loose for months, eventually being found in Middlesbrough.

The two defendants stood together in Leeds on 9 December 1903 and they stood before Mr Justice Darling, a man who had been involved in the trial of Oscar Wilde and who was to try, only a few weeks after this, the infamous 'baby farmers' Sachs and Walters. The only flimsy shred of an argument in favour of Gallagher was that he had been drinking on the day he killed Swann and, of course, that his motives were a reprisal, a strong urge to administer some 'justice' of his own. In the events of that day, inside the home, there had undoubtedly been some incitement to kill, and Darling knew this. He said to Emily: 'As for the woman, it is my duty to tell you that one does not commit murder only with one's hands. If one person instigates another to commit murder, and that person does it, the instigator is also guilty of murder.'

It took only half an hour for the jury to find both of them guilty of wilful murder. But there was a strange twist to this tale, because there was a vital piece of evidence which Darling did not mention before the jury retired. It turned out that Emily's part in the killing was far more than incitement. Gallagher had said, after being arrested, that Emily had used a poker to hit her husband with and that Gallagher did not touch the dead man. Did this mean that Emily hit her husband after he was dead? All that mattered was that Justice Darling believed her to have been actively involved in the killing of William Swann.

The fact that the verdict was decided without a report of what Gallagher had said about the poker has to say something significant about the feeling concerning Emily's state of mind at the time. After all, people had heard her say that Johnny should kill her husband, and that is all that was required to convince the twelve good men and true in Leeds that day.

But there is another perspective on Emily Swann: one of understanding and compassion and, paradoxically, this comes substantially from the man who hanged her: John Ellis. The bare facts of Emily's fate were given in *The Times* of 29 December 1903:

> *The Wombwell Murderers – The Home Secretary has declined to interfere in the case of the Wombwell murderers, Emily Swann and John Gallagher, who were found guilty at Leeds Assizes of the wilful murder of the female prisoner's husband. They will be executed at 9 o'clock this morning.*

But Ellis is the man who saw the woman inside that supposed murderous beast who broke the laws of nature. He saw a forty-two-year-old woman, '. . . a little, stumpy, round-faced woman, only 4 feet 10 inches tall and 122 lbs in weight. She was the first condemned woman I had ever seen and, frankly, I didn't think the authorities would allow her to go to the scaffold.' He was wrong, and it affected him greatly.

The couple were told that the reprieve had been dismissed and, from that moment, Ellis saw in Emily Swann a woman who was emotionally wrecked. He said: 'When she was told of

Armley Gaol. Laura Carter

the Home Office decision it absolutely staggered her, and she wore a look of utter misery when I peeped in at her that evening.'

The reality Ellis saw was a tiny woman, one who had had to suffer violence for years, had been beaten, shouted at, despised and humiliated and now. after finding that there had been an opportunity for sheer animal revenge, a momentary release of hatred, as a mad dog would turn on its master after being kicked and beaten, she had become a small, weak woman once more, being asked to accept the reality that someone was going to hang her, inside a miserable gaol.

Ellis's tone is one of gentleness and, as we read his memoir, we notice how observant he was – how he saw the wardresses becoming friendly with their female charge and how both prisoners showed 'religious penitence'. The hangman's account of the deaths of the two lovers is painful reading. Gallagher was first to the scaffold after being pinioned and then a white hood was placed over his head, when Emily came to stand behind him he didn't see her. She simply said: 'Good morning John.' He was shocked and replied: 'Good morning, love.'

As the rope was put around Emily's neck she said: 'Goodbye. God bless you!' According to Ellis, she had gone from being a squirming emotional wreck on the floor of her cell to someone quite stoical, and a glass of brandy was all it took. Her two wardresses had broken down and were very upset, just as Emily bucked up and gave a smile of acceptance of her situation.

The entire story, through modern eyes, provides a mix that is difficult to accept: here is a classic, almost elemental *ménage à trois*, with all the concomitant enmity and jealousy, with a last act to equal a grand tragedy, except that it was finally also sordid and demeaning, in that the killing was pointless and brutal, in spite the husband's former cruelty. Central to the process of the story, all the way through, was the fact that many public statements were made, almost to the extent of a running commentary on the macabre events of that horrendously determined killing. It was as if the killer, the man directly responsible, was working very hard to show how effectively he was dispensing some kind of 'natural justice' in beating to death the wife-beater.

CHAPTER 16

The Tragedy of Mrs Castle: Driffield
1923

Oh, my poor bairns!

In February 1923, Mrs Grace Castle put her three children in the bath at her home in Market Place. As if possessed and driven by an inner voice, she forced their heads under the water and drowned them. Three children, the oldest only seven, were found just before midnight that night when police arrived. It has to have been one of the most tragic events in the chronicles of Yorkshire murder. In fact, the very word murder is paradoxically unfitting. Poor Grace Castle was in need of help; her mind was deranged and she had allowed a terrible voice of unreason and destruction to creep into her being.

On that horrendous evening, she had tried to ring her husband, Fred, who was at a Freemasons' meeting. But there had been no telephone there. Circumstances conspired that evening to lead the woman to kill. Her husband was a good man, and had fought in the Great War, coming home to work as a brewer's manager at the Market Place. He had also been a well-known local footballer, playing for Driffield and for Cranswick. Not only did Grace kill her sons, but she tried to take her own life as well, taking a tincture of iodine. The poignant situation here was that, in her mind, she had killed the family 'for him'.

When the police officer arrived, Grace Castle was sitting in the kitchen in a state of mental turmoil, saying: 'Oh, Mr Waind, you don't know why I have done it!' Why she had done it is difficult to explain but these are her own words were, in a piece she wrote in her notebook:

Whatever happens, don't spend a penny on me. I am cursed and so are my children. The only way I was to have saved their souls

*was to have killed them ... Now I cannot see a way out at all.
My husband is the best father and a fine man. He worships his
children and what a disappointment for him to have seen them
grow up in desperation and crime ...*

An insight into her condition was provided by the maid in the
house, Alice Harper, who was with Mrs Castle earlier that
evening. She said that the children were put to bed at about a
quarter to eight, but that when they were asleep, Grace was in
pain. Alice thought she was suffering from her usual neuralgia.
But everyone managed to get to bed, and Alice was roused from
her sleep at eleven-thirty and she saw Grace sitting in the
kitchen saying that her head felt funny and then she said: 'Oh
my poor bairns!'

The first meeting of the coroner's inquest was a brief affair and
was swiftly adjourned. Thomas Holtby, the coroner, summed
up the feeling at the time when he said that the deaths con-
stituted the 'saddest tragedy' he had come across. The inquest
was adjourned until medical evidence became available. The
Reverend George Storer presided at the funeral of the children.
Grace Castle was charged with murder, having malice aforethought, and, of course, was guilty of attempted suicide as well.

At the resumed inquest, some medical evidence was presented from the family doctor, Dr Keith, a man who had fought
alongside Fred Castle in the war. He confirmed that Grace had
suffered from some kind of nervous condition for six months.
Keith had attended on the night of the deaths and there he
found that she had taken the iodine simply because it was
something 'chemical', as it was hardly the type of substance a
person would take if they wanted to die quickly. All she could
say was that the doctor would see by her writings why she had
done it. She was totally distracted and, although aware of what
she had done and how she had killed her children, it was all
somehow unreal to her, outside her range of comprehension.

She was detained in Hull Gaol to await her trial, and, at this
point the journalists had begun to be annoyingly insensitive and
intrusive, so much so that a member of the jury requested that
he make a statement on this, saying that he wished to express
his strong disapproval of the flash-lights and cameras being
used. Through modern eyes, there is nothing unusual or unex-

pected in this, but in 1923, the moral climate was more rigid and especially in the quieter areas in the provinces, a 'big story' in the eyes of a journalist out to make a name for himself was far from how it was – it was a terrible local sadness.

At York Assizes, in March 1923, Dr Howlett, the prison doctor in Hull, was called to give an assessment of Grace's condition. He confirmed what Dr Simpson, the Medical Superintendent of the East Riding, had said, that though Grace could put into words the sequence of events on that tragic night, she was unable to feel any emotion or derive any meaning from this. Consequently, both medical men agreed that she was insane. In fact, Simpson noted that it was a case of 'long-standing insanity'.

Her youngest son, Kenneth, had been only three, and it was noted during the investigation that Grace Castle had been 'in a poor state of health' since Kenneth's birth. As clues to why she chose to kill in this way and for the reasons given, we can theorise that her reasons were partly altruistic – thinking that the one she loved would be better for the lack of stress caused by worry about the children, and also that her own problems (depression) would be alleviated. The tincture of opium is an interesting detail, because it bears no relation to any substance used commonly in these contexts. The hallmark of desperation and irrational thought. It also seems highly likely that Grace was suffering from post-natal depression and, in the circumstances in which she had to live, little was done to address this. The spirit of the times was to press on regardless. Even with a maid and help around the house, Grace was still under pressure, and she bore a deep well of unhappiness within her.

Grace Castle was therefore unfit to plead and was admitted to Broadmoor on 9 March 1923. The historian Helen Stewart has tried to follow up the future course of the Castles' lives but little has emerged. A man who went to the funeral of the children recalled that Fred Castle had been ill in later life, and had remained a Freemason, but as to Grace, we know nothing of her later life and her ultimate fate remains a mystery.

In Driffield Cemetery the gravestone can still be seen, giving testimony to one of the most melancholy stories ever told about murders within a family. There it is recorded that Donald, Hubert and Kenneth Castle rest in peace and that their deaths were 'in tragic circumstances'.

CHAPTER 17

Louie Calvert
1925

It was all brutality and lies with her and she was clever with it . . .

Lily Waterhouse was forty years old in 1923, when Louie Calvert knocked on her door. Lily's husband had died a year before, and she had lived in Amberley Road for fourteen years. She had no idea that Calvert had come to stay with her as part of a ruse to fool her husband, Arty, into thinking that she was with her sister in Dewsbury, and that she was having a baby. Louie Calvert was indulging in one of her complex deceptions, as she was not only leading a life of deep ambiguity, but she was a person who enjoyed lying so that she could get the thrills of escape from the mundane life.

Louie had been housekeeper for a Mr Frobisher the year before this, and that man was found dead in the River Aire in July 1922. With hindsight it seems peculiar that the coroner did not ask more questions about this corpse. There was a wound on the back of his head and he had no boots on. At the inquest, little Louie appeared and stated that she had pawned the boots for a few shillings. All this was very strange because Frobisher lived a mile or so away from where his body was found. Had he walked barefoot to his death? Was it suicide? It is astounding that the verdict recorded at the inquest was death by mis-adventure.

That had been the first appearance of Louie Calvert in the records, and she was destined to be far more prominent than that. She moved on from Frobisher's place to marry Arty Calvert in Hunslet, and now there she was, away from home, pretending to be pregnant. She had two children already, one living with Arty and her, Kenneth; and a girl, Annie, who lived in Dewsbury. So here then was a strange situation: a woman of thirty-three turning up, wanting a room, and then, unknown to

Amberley Road, where Calvert killed. Laura Carter

the landlady, the guest was trying to work out how to possess a baby that she could pass off as her own. The obvious thing to do was to advertise, as you would for any goods. The advert in the Leeds paper did indeed work.

A teenager from Pontefract had given birth to a little girl in Leeds and her mother saw Louie's advert. It did not take long to arrange for an adoption; all Louie had to do was lie low in her lodgings and wait until the baby was delivered to her. In this phase of her life we see Louie Calvert, the odd performer, acting a role in the community. The situation was extremely bizarre: here was a married woman living under an assumed identity in another part of the city to that in which her husband and real home were, pretending to be there in order to care for her newborn, currently in hospital. Yet strangely that would have

seemed a plausible tale; at the time many young babies were ill
with all kinds of maladies, from diphtheria to scarlet fever.
Clearly, many would have been in hospital in intensive care,
and the mother would visit.

Louie's love of performance, of escaping from herself and
going into a role, was changing. Formerly, when she worked for
Frobisher, she wore Salvation Army clothes and acted the part
well. But, as if her life were a feature in a B movie of the time,
deception led to more problems at Lily Waterhouse's home.
This also sprang from the fact that Louie was a compulsive
thief, and her pawning of Frobisher's boots had been just one of
many visits to the pawnbroker's with items stolen. Another
startling aspect of Louie Calvert is that, though she was very
short and thin, in fact under five feet tall, her personality was
forceful and assertive. She was capable of instilling fear in
people, using sheer egoistic control and toughness. So much
was this evident to Lily Waterhouse that she was at first fright-
ened to say anything when she began to notice that various
objects had disappeared from her home.

But she gathered some determination when she found pawn
tickets clearly relating to the objects missing. This was a time, of
course, when many working people were in dire straits and
habits such as pawning a best Sunday suit almost on a weekly
basis was one desperate way of keeping a little ready cash in
the house. Louie was reported to the police and was in court
answering charges, but she returned to her lodgings, packed her
bags and her baby, and went home to Calverts' house in Railway Place, Hunslet. As earlier writers on the amazing dimin-
utive Calvert have speculated, how on earth she managed to be
so prominent and sociable around Leeds in the time she was
supposed to be having a child in Dewsbury is amazing; she was
a familiar sight to many, and being distinctive in her build and
her speech, she would have been seen by people passing from
one area of Leeds to another, perhaps commuting.

But before Louie Calvert was to leave to go home to her husband, she had some business to attend to in Amberley Road,
and it was a deadly affair. It was all brutality and lies with her,
and she was clever with it.

It was just before Easter when Louie left Lily Waterhouse
home, and Lily had been seen going into her house one

Wednesday night around that time. But in those terraces neighbours saw and heard a great deal; there was very little privacy and people were sensitive to any unusual sounds. Domestic arguments would be heard by several neighbours, for instance. On this occasion, a neighbour heard noises in the lodger's room and then saw Louie as she left the house, carrying her baby. She told the neighbour that Lily was upset, but that she (Louie) was going home. She explained the odd noises by lying that she and Lily had been moving a bed.

At last Arty Calvert had his wife back, and also what he thought was his baby, little Dorothy. This was a happy time of course, and they were up late. But the next morning, Arty saw that there was some luggage in the house that had not been there the night before. Unbelievably, Louie Calvert had returned to Amberley Road in the early hours and had collected this large suitcase. At this stage in her career, Louie was clumsy. She was seen by several people, despite the early time of day, and these sightings would be valuable statements later on in the tale. Even more surprisingly as we re-read the case today, Louie left a note. If she had not done that, then the chances are that the dual life she had constructed may well have kept her anonymous when the police started looking for the little woman who had lodged in Amberley Road.

They did indeed start looking for her, very soon after her dawn appearance at the lodgings, and this was because Lily Waterhouse had, of course, started a paper trail for the police when she summonsed her tenant. When Lily did not appear for that, the police came to check on her. What they found in her home was the woman's corpse, lying on the floor in a bedroom. There was plenty of her blood in evidence around the body, even to the extent that some had splashed on the wall. She had been battered on the head, as there was dried blood clotted on her scalp.

The hallmark was there at the scene, though it was not perceived at the time: Lily Waterhouse was fully dressed – apart from her boots. There had been a violent struggle and the old lady had fought with some tenacity, as she was badly bruised, and it had taken several heavy blows to finish her. It is somewhat difficult to accept, bearing in mind the physical stature of Louie, that Lily Waterhouse had also been strangled. The killer, the police noticed, had cut up cloth to use to tie Lily's hands and feet; yet there must have been something else used to strangle the woman as the ligature marks on her neck were wider than that caused by a strip of cloth. It is a gruesome thought that the noises heard by the neighbours were almost certainly the movements of the dying woman's limbs as she was shaking in her death-throes. Her murderous lodger, small though she was, had bound her tight, in an effort to stop the noises made by her feet; neighbours would certainly have heard the sounds, and would have come to ask questions. One important detail here is that the room was not carpeted. The sounds of feet thrashing on wooden floorboards could surely have meant that the murderer would have been disturbed as people responded to the noises heard through paper-thin walls.

What has read previously as the image of a widow leading a lonely and rather impoverished lifestyle, as questions were asked in the ensuing investigation, turned out to be something very different. In fact, some of Lily's previous lodgers hade been ladies of the night. These were tough times in Leeds and there was high unemployment. A widow with a low income would no doubt have been tempted to take in guests who would pay well, and no questions would be asked. But Lily was also unusual in that she had not been the isolated figure one might suppose. She had, since her husband's death, had lots of visitors and had lived quite an interesting life, including some dabbling in spiritualism. Neighbours, answering questions about her character, seemed eager to mention the shadier side of Lily's life, even to the point of one commenting that 'She was not a clean woman.' Understandably, these comments and implications about the victim led the police to seek suspects among the clientele she had mixed with in the recent past.

But then people began to recall the lodger with the baby, and there was also the matter of the letter Louie had left. It was the letter about the deceit over the birth supposedly in Dewsbury. As this was addressed to Mrs Louie Calvert, there was a lead there. She was soon to be tracked down, and this woman who had been enjoying the strange thrills of moving from one name and identity to another for some time, escaping the reality she perhaps feared, opened her door one night in April 1925 to find Detective Inspector Pass standing there. As has been remarked previously, Louie was an unprepossessing sight, and there was a terrible irony in the fact that one of her assumed names had been Edith Thompson, the celebrated poisoner who had been hanged at Holloway in 1923. The irony is that whereas Edith Thompson was sophisticated and articulate, with a real presence, little Louie Calvert was ill-looking, underweight and coarse. Amazingly, Louie was wearing Mrs Waterhouse's boots when she answered the door. The beginning of the end for her criminal career was at hand.

The police work was extremely efficient; after Louie had 'covered up' the murder when she went to the Waterhouse home with a response of both nonchalance and surprise, saying, 'Oh, did she do herself in then?' the police went to work on the adoption and the Dewsbury connection. Louie was arrested and taken away, and at that point we have to speculate about poor Kenneth and Arty Calvert. Arty had just learned that his baby was not his at all, and was now wondering why his wife was in the police station. Poor little Kenneth was without his mother. At the town hall, Arty learned all the real facts for the first time, and while he was absorbing all that, Louie was insisting that, when charged with murder, she didn't do it.

The trial at Leeds was before Mr Justice Wright. The court learned that for the two years before she moved in with Calvert, Louie had lived hand-to-mouth, but had realised that there were ways of exploiting poverty and existing in various roles and guises. Possibly one of the most interesting and informative of these was her time as a Salvation Army woman. But it is futile to seek for any deep religious feeling in this woman; the feeling generally is that they looked after her, and the organisation was easy for her to exploit. She went to Alpha Street Hall meetings, but it was all a front. Often, small details speak volumes and in this case, it has to be noted that she had even stolen her bonnet from a Salvation Army member. The author of the most exhaustive account of this case has mentioned a neighbour who knew Louie well, and she testified that the little woman had violent tempers, and that she was capable of changing her mood rapidly, and of using bad language. The witness said that the obscenities from Calvert were so extreme that she had banned her from coming into her home.

Leeds Town Hall, where Arty Calvert learned the truth behind his wife's lies.
Author's collection

It is pathetically banal to report that when Louie Calvert was asked if she had anything to say before the sentence was passed, she said simply: 'Yes, Sir, I'm pregnant.' There is something profoundly informative about that statement. It indicates the naïve facility she had for a child-like defence when cornered. Saying an infantile thing like that was tantamount to admitting that her sense of reality was very slender and her inner fantasy, feeding the outer criminal who was a predator in the streets of Leeds, was a truly frightening aspect of her.

Then something occurred that had happened many times, perhaps most famously in the case of Mary Bateman (see Chapter 8): because Louie had constantly avoided any statements in the witness box with the argument that she was ill, and now supposedly pregnant, a medical inspection was essential. Dr Hoyland Smith went to examine her in the court cell and, as with Bateman, a woman had to attend. This woman was from a jury of mothers selected for the purpose. But the difficulty was in keeping with Louie's muddled and crazy career: there was no proof either way.

The result was that the death sentence was passed. A Leeds City Councillor said at the time that he felt pity for her and added: 'She was a thin, wan-looking creature, only weighing a few stone. I should never legislate on the lines of hanging a woman.' But others soon realised that there were two Louie Calverts. In the dock she had been quiet, restrained and polite. But down in the cell she shouted abuse at her husband, trying to say that he was to blame. All he could say was: 'It can't be helped lass.' Other interpretations of her actions and responses to graphic descriptions of the attack on Lily Waterhouse, and of the corpse, indicate that she was unfeeling and mentally distant from any sense of the events unfolding being in any way 'real'.

But the woman, who was seen by some as undersized and pathetic, had done the awful deed, and of course she had also been wily and cunning in the extreme. Her actions in court and before the magistrate when first charged show an amount of guile too. She dressed in black and to the local reporters she became 'the woman in black'. It has been noted that she fussed over her appearance, as if she were still putting on clothes to be someone else – to project a persona which was not really her. In the magistrates' court, even as evidence was being spoken, she changed her hat, putting on a black silk one instead of her everyday mauve.

There was an appeal. In London, she was again dressed all in black, and the context at the time was a difficult one with regard to the hanging of women. Since the notorious Thompson case in 1923, the eight women given a death sentence had all been reprieved. It must have looked to many that this was going to be the case yet again, as a petition had been signed by 3,000 people. Much was made in the press on the topic of her child – the question of what would happen to her, and who might adopt her, was something that sold papers.

A factor in the appeal was that Louie was not pregnant. There was also nothing else that was new. In spite of the media interest in the case and in the very emotive issue of hanging a woman, the sentence was not quashed. The end was in sight for her then; relatives came to pay a last visit to her in the cell. She actually wrote a letter on her last night on Earth and in this she said: 'I am keeping up quite well and you will have the joy of meeting me in Heaven, for I am quite ready and prepared to meet my God.'

Finally, this enigmatic woman who had fuelled her life with lies, confessed the crime to the warders, and she also said, after clearly being troubled by something that was on her conscience, that she had murdered another victim – an old man she used to work for as his housekeeper. It comes as no surprise to us now, with hindsight, that this man was Frobisher, the man found in the canal, without his boots. Some might argue that this was a lie, though; that she was again fantasising. The whole question of why she removed boots from the bodies of her victims relates to this same deep personality in which complex problems existed, maybe even to deviance in the removal of the boots, with a sexual undertone. But more likely, boots were some kind of comfort in a harsh world of pawnbrokers and poverty.

Of course, if she did kill Frobisher, there must have been a way to overcome to obvious obstacles to achieving this. After all, if he was thrown into the water at Monk Bridge on the Aire, then she would most likely have killed him close to the river, or else how could such a tiny woman have conveyed the corpse to the river? If he was killed next to the river, he could have been rolled in after his boots had been removed. Alternatively, if she killed him in Mercy Street and then somehow had the corpse taken to the riverside, that would not be totally impossible, but most unlikely. Though it has to be pointed out that Mercy Street was only around 400 yards from the water, off Wellington Street.

Louie Calvert was said to have gone to her death 'more bravely than many men'. One has to say that surely there was something man-like in her; as Shakespeare said of Lady Macbeth: 'Bring forth men children only . . .' There was an element of Louie Calvert that had that quality of brutal, unfeeling detachment we see in serial killers, but very rarely in women, even of that category.

She was executed at Strangeways Prison in Manchester on 26 June 1926.

Chapter 18

A Lover's Knife
1925

I have done it – it is because
I love him.

On 10 January 1925, in a Bradford street, Douglas Hodgkins saw a man and a woman quarrelling as they walked along. He heard the woman say that she would 'not be humbugged by him any more'. It could have been like any other lovers' row, but then the woman took a knife from her handbag and stabbed the man in the chest. She did that incredible act of hatred and then dissolved into sheer panic, shouting that they needed to get the man to hospital. People heard her screaming, 'If I have done it, it is because I love him.'

The woman was Catherine Thorpe and the man she stabbed was a musician, Herbert Musgrave. Both were married, Catherine (known as Kitty) was twenty-six and Musgrave only twenty-three. Catherine was living apart from her husband and trying to hold down a job. She met Herbert Musgrave one night at the *Grosvenor Hotel* and they grew close.

In her defence, Catherine Thorpe said that they were always in each other's company that month, December 1924, and Musgrave had promised to help her and, as it was expressed at the hearing at the magistrates' court, 'to take her into rooms as a permanent arrangement'. But there was always a strain in their relationship and this odd, puzzling character borrowed money from 'Kitty' (Catherine Thorpe). He would not pay the debt and at first that was said to be a factor in her desire to harm him.

At the inquest, a verdict of wilful murder was returned by Mr J G Hutchinson, who saw no complications in the events of that night at all. The knife had come from a butcher's shop, and everyone who had spoken to the police had been convinced that

MURDER VERDICT AGAINST A WOMAN.

"GUILTY UNDER GREAT PROVOCATION."

At the Leeds Assizes yesterday CATHERINE THORPE, 21, was tried for the wilful murder of Herbert Musgrove, a musician, at Bradford on January 10. The accused pleaded "Not Guilty." The jury, after an absence of 30 minutes, returned a verdict of "Guilty under great provocation," and with a strong recommendation to mercy. The prisoner collapsed on being sentenced to death by MR. JUSTICE BRANSON, and was carried out of Court unconscious.

Opening the case for the Crown, Mr. F. MITCHELL INNES, K.C., said the murder of Musgrove was in the ordinary sense of the words deliberate and premeditated. The prisoner was a married woman living apart from her husband and the dead man was married living apart from his wife.

Douglas Hodgkins said that on Saturday, January 10, he saw the prisoner, accompanied by a man, coming along quarrelling. The woman said she would not "be humbugged with him any longer." She took a knife from her handbag and stabbed the man in the neck. Afterwards she became hysterical, shouting for people to take Musgrove to the hospital. Later she said, "If I have done it, it is because I love him."

The prisoner, giving evidence for the defence, said her marriage was unhappy and she went out to earn her living. She met Musgrove at the Grosvenor Hotel in December, and afterwards went out with him almost every night. She was fond of him, and he promised to take her into rooms as a permanent arrangement. She had some trouble with Musgrove over money that she had lent to him, but he would not repay her. When she met him on the night of January 10 she had the knife with her, intending only to frighten him. He complained that he was in danger of losing his employment on account of her and called her a foul name and pushed her. There was a struggle, and she did not know how the knife had touched him. She never struck him a blow, and had no intention of doing him any injury. "I could not live without him," she added.

The Times report on the Thorpe case. Author's collection

the attack had been premeditated and there was an intent to kill. Hutchinson stated plainly: 'the blow was not struck when she was in a sudden passion'.

In the street argument that fateful night, Musgrave had said that he was going to lose his job because of her behaviour, swore at her, and they struggled. Then, Kitty Thorpe said: 'I did not know how the knife had touched him.' This reads as a very feeble account of what happened, not at all like Mr Hodgkins' memory of the altercation. She said that she could not live without him. This was at Leeds Assizes, where people supporting her had gathered some cash to pay for a decent barrister. They had Mr Cawthorn to represent her at the magistrates' court, and she pleaded not guilty. At that first hearing, a detective had stated that he was present when Thorpe was at the infirmary and that she 'smelled of drink'. Dr Niven was also present and saw that she was hysterical. She fainted at one point, then recovered and the doctor said that she was recovering from too much alcohol; he said, 'her breath smelled of drink and she was rather sullen in her manner'.

What she did say, again, to the police officer was that she couldn't bear to think that Musgrave was dead. 'Don't say he is dead ... If I've done it, it's because I loved him.'

After the evidence had been heard in court in Leeds, the jury brought in a verdict of guilty but 'under great provocation'. They recommended mercy, but the judge, Mr Justice Branson, put on the black cap and Thorpe was sentenced to hang. Kitty Thorpe then collapsed into unconsciousness was carried from the court.

Later that year in the court of criminal appeal, Mr C J Frankland represented Thorpe before Mr Justice Avory, a man of whom it was said that in his court, the guilty quaked and the innocent rejoiced. Which would it be for the woman who stood there, hoping to escape the noose? Frankland's basis for appeal was that there had been a large amount of evidence that there had been extreme provocation in the matter, and that the facts relating to a defence of manslaughter had not been put forward. Despite the fact that details relating to manslaughter were not integral to the defence put forward in Leeds, the appeal went on. Mitchell-Innes, for the Crown, said that there was no issue of manslaughter. It was going to be a tough ordeal for all concerned.

Avory stressed that the lifestyle of the dead man was a factor, as he was pointing out the morality at the heart of the matter; Musgrave had played piano in Bradford pubs. He was married and had two children, yet he was separated from his life. There was a strong undercurrent of moral comment there. The narrative of the two young people's affair was important. Thorpe lived with her mother (who was divorced) and she had had a child when she was only eighteen. But the hard fact was that Kitty Thorpe had told several people on the day before the attack that she was going to knife Musgrave. The way she expressed this was that she was 'going to do someone in'. This was one of the most peculiar aspects of this case, and the context of the people and places to whom Kitty Thorpe spoke about the murder is one suggesting more a deranged mind than and intention to coldly kill. She had told one person she would 'do it on'. This is a rather muddled expression, and she was maybe in drink at that point.

What, then, was the basis for the claim of manslaughter? In the Leeds trial, all that had been recorded was a small element in Thorpe's statement that Musgrave had pushed and jostled her. This had been extended into something closer to actual

Sir Rufus Isaacs. Clifford Elmer

abuse. The basis of the appeal was on that, and it was hoped that the details given would amount to some kind of provocation. This was the only hope, as the manslaughter issue was soon dismissed.

Lord Reading, in his contribution to the debate, said: 'It is not, in our opinion, correct to say that there was no alternative but to find accident or murder.' He added that, in the instance of the suggested abuse, there was 'no blow was struck, there were used to her words of reproach, accompanied by pushing and jostling'.

Avory pointed out that: 'In the present case, the evidence on which it was suggested that the defence of manslaughter ought to have been left to the jury was a fraction of Thorpe's evidence in which she said that Musgrave abused her ...'. The conclusion was that there was no evidence of that, and it should not have been left to the jury in Leeds. All that was left was the crucial word 'mercy' as recommended by the jury. Fortunately for Kitty Thorpe, mercy was given her and she had her sentence commuted to penal servitude for life.

CHAPTER 19

A Hired Assassin
1962

He was found battered and strangled by his motorbike ...

On 18 October, 1962, Leslie Hutchinson was on his motorbike in Hessle, not far from his place of business (a smallholding), when the bike hit a stretched line of wire and he was thrown from the machine. But it wasn't the fall that killed him: he was found battered and strangled by his motorbike and the enquiry began.

Just before Christmas that year three people stood in the dock at Beverley. They were Marjorie Hutchinson, the widow of the dead man, aged thirty-nine, Roy Bigby, thirty-five, and Charles Green, thirty-four. It was a special sitting of the magistrates and they were listening to expert reports given from tests on the wire. One of the most significant details at that time in Beverley was the fact that there were two life insurance policies taken out on Leslie Hutchinson's life. One was for over £207 and the other for £1,056 – a policy to cover the mortgage on the house in Hessle.

The court heard a police constable called Kettley talk about a test in which he had driven a motorbike at a low speed of 6 mph at a length of wire. He reported that this made him lose control and that without sticking his legs out, he would have been thrown off. He also added that the bike in question was not in a good condition and in need of a service. This hearing was just the beginning of an intriguing case.

The son of the family, Leslie Hutchinson, aged nineteen, was present. He was in for a hard time and it began at this juncture, with his having to testify with regard to some handwriting. He had initially said that it was his mother's writing but then he changed his mind and said it was his father's. This small detail

THE WEIR, HESSLE.
NEAR HULL.

"SCOTT" SERIES. NO. 457.

Hessle at he time of this case. Author's collection

indicates the pressure on the young man in such awful circumstances. The public would have to wait for the full account of this case, as the three were committed for trial in Leeds.

Marjorie Hutchinson pleaded not guilty.

In Leeds, Mrs Hutchinson's defence was that she admitted to conspiring with Bigby and Green to assault, but not to murder. She was before Mr Justice Melford Stevenson, who directed the jury to disregard her answer.

Who is?
Kenneth Green?

Kenneth Green. Hull Daily Mail

Not guilty to murder meant that she was in for a hard time. Bigby, who was given to be 'her lover', pleaded not guilty. But Green had pleaded guilty and had already been sentenced to life imprisonment. The neighbours in Buttfield Road, Hessle, must have had a lot to talk about now that there was high drama in their midst.

The prosecution was led by Henry Scott, and he started to probe into the imagined scenario of Green being hired as an

assassin, and that he had placed the wire close to Mr Hutchinson's kennels, then approached the injured man on the ground, battered him and strangled him until he was dead. For her defence, Marjorie's lawyer, Rudolph Lyons, did his best to develop the notion that she had wanted to have her husband beaten up rather than killed:

> **Mr Lyons:** What did you intend should be done to your husband?
> **Mrs Hutchinson:** A good hiding, Mr Lyons.
> **Mr Lyons:** Did you ever intend more than that?
> **Mrs Hutchinson:** No.
> **Mr Lyons:** Did you at any time intend to desire more than that?
> **Mrs Hutchinson:** No.
> **Mr Lyons:** Did you ever instruct Green to kill him?
> **Mrs Hutchinson:** No.

The basis of the defence was that there was a domestic violence situation; that Leslie Hutchinson 'knocked her about' and also that he was having an affair. Marjorie said that her marriage was a very unhappy one and that she thought that a beating might change things. That seems a hopelessly stupid thing to say at any time by anyone, but she said: 'I wanted him to have a good hiding for his treatment of me – not out of revenge but in the hope that it might alter him.'

Marjorie Hutchinson. Hull Daily Mail

Lyons was determined to make the most of this, and stressed the idea that she had been a good wife in spite of her wandering husband. He asked if she still loved him 'in spite of what he had done?' She affirmed this, and then Lyons asked a clever question: 'What were you hoping for in the future?'

Marjorie replied: 'Happiness'.

The defence meant that Marjorie was expected to explain the situation of abuse and to give examples: she did this, particularly referring to a time when Green had seen what

Leslie Hutchinson. Hull Daily Mail

damage Leslie Hutchinson had done to Marjorie and he offered to beat him up for £50. We have to reflect on the oddity of that. What kind of man would want paying for such an act? It must have seemed peculiar to judge and jury that a man who was close to the woman wanted payment for something that was, however wrong-headed, supposedly a move to change the situation.

She had to explain the fateful day, and her story was that she expected both Green and her lover to be there that day near the kennels where her husband had a dog-breeding business: 'I thought that Roy was going to help get Les off the bike and Green was going to give him a good hiding. I did not know a weapon was going to be used. I did not see Green with any weapon and I definitely would not have taken him there if I had known he was going to use piping with lead in it.' This indicates the appeal for sympathy in a somewhat desperate way, and to this was added the fact that she was pregnant and by her husband. The point not to be missed was that she had 'taken him there' (meaning Bigby). In other words, there was a planned collusion to do serious harm. What she called a 'good hiding' was grievous bodily harm – and that is a twin concept with murder in such cases, reaching back to mid-Victorian legislation.

The 'good hiding' was in fact a vicious attack with included giving the victim a dozen thumps with the lead piping and then – and this is the detail that sent Green to prison for life – Hutchinson was strangled by the belt from his own boiler suit.

On 6 February the verdict was given, and Marjorie Hutchinson was found guilty of murder. Bigby was given a three-year sentence and she received a life sentence. It was a tough time for the jury; they took over four hours to reach their verdict and

The arrest of Marjorie Hutchinson. Hull Daily Mail

Police searching near where the body was found. Hull Daily Mail

Judge Stevenson said that they had had 'labour of exceptional severity'. In a case in which the judge took more than usual care of the twelve people in the box, he said that they were to be excluded from the jury ballot for the next ten years.

Melford Stevenson summed up the case in these words, addressing Bigby:

I cannot shut my eyes to the fact that you leant yourself to a dreadful conspiracy with your co-defendant and with the man Green. On the view which the jury have taken you did not intend the hideous consequences which the execution of that conspiracy had. Nevertheless, you must pay the penalty for a grievous and dreadful offence.

Marjorie Hutchinson faced life imprisonment.

CHAPTER 20

Taxi Driver Killing
1972

... he had been shot once through the forehead at point-blank range.

People out late at night in the summer of 1972 in Halifax found it hard to find a taxi, and when they did, they would find themselves up against all kinds of security measures. The reason for this was that on 24 March that year, Milton Walker, a taxi driver, left for work in his white Ford Cortina and never returned. His burning car was later found in Batley early the next day and his body was found, hands and feet tied and a bullet in his head, on the moors in Denshaw. A sawn-off shotgun was found at the scene as well. These discoveries were made five days after the car was found in flames.

It would be logical for the response to that manner of death to be one of a hitman killing' done with professionalism and a certain ruthless efficiency. Or equally, to think that it had some characteristics of the ritualistic murders we associate with serial killers. It was certainly callous and brutal.

The alleged killers, John and Shirley Reed, were tracked down and in November they stood in the dock as Leeds Assizes charged with murder. They were from Oldham. John was thirty-three and Shirley only twenty-one. But the trial in Leeds was to have an element of mystery, even after the sentence had been passed. They were jailed for life by Mr Justice Nield, John Reed for a minimum of twenty years.

Shirley Reed collapsed in court and had to receive medical attention, being eventually taken from the court sobbing, an emotional wreck. But John Reed denied that he was guilty and his lawyer stated that there would be an appeal. The mystery comes in when it is recalled that the lawyer in question, Jack

Levi, stated that he had received an anonymous letter from a woman and that this contained 'information that could be material to the defence'. Levi added that he would like to hear more from the writer of the letter, and an appeal for this person to come forward was made to the press.

Time passed before anything substantial emerged, but by October 1973, police decided to have a new enquiry into the case after the court of appeal had made a decision to carry this into effect. John Reed had, controversially, cancelled his appeal application. John had given a long statement, and the lawyer for Shirley said that this statement might be an optimistic development for Shirley too, as it 'explained matters hitherto left unexplained'.

But the case was to become one in which John Reed took centre stage and Shirley faded into the background, eventually being released. Why the man figured most in this was that, in 1980, his case was supposed to be referred to the European Court of Human Rights. There is no trace of this ever having happened, and records of Shirley Reed's fate are also very sparse. The whole story appears to have faded away, and that is a mystery greater than the real story of what went on in the Milton Walker killing. It almost seems like a conspiracy of silence around the case, and we still do not know for sure what Shirley Reed's part in this killing was.

CHAPTER 21

'A Sad History' and a Murder 1980

I hope they win the freedom I have got.

n November 1980, a woman was released from jail, and given a two-year suspended sentence. From her home, Mrs Joyce Fuller said something very powerful and emotional in support of two Yorkshire sisters for whom she felt a particular sympathy. She said: 'I hope they win the freedom I have got.' Mrs Fuller had lived a life of terrible abuse, being beaten by her husband repeatedly and over a long period. Finally, she had attacked the man and stabbed him to death. She was charged with manslaughter, and the judge, Mr Justice Chapman, said, 'There is no necessity for me to add to the troubles you have brought upon yourself by sending you to prison.'

There had also been pressure groups at work and statements made by MPs on the Leeds case. Mrs Fuller spoke out, the young women were in Askham Grange Prison. So what had they done?

Annette and Charlene Maw had lived in fear of their drunken father, Thomas. The sisters had witnessed him severely assault their mother, Beryl, in their Bradford home. There were two girls and a boy in the family; the father, Thomas, was relentlessly violent. His behaviour was totally reprehensible. One day he even went so far as to approach prostitutes when he was actually with his wife. To recount his chronicle of cruelty is to record actions beyond belief – horrendous brutality and torture of the worst kind. Perhaps the nature of his sick mind is best observed when we note that one day he killed the pet rabbit of the house and then forced the children to eat the animal. The worst excesses of Nazi pseudo-science could rank alongside his worst deeds, as he behaved much as a cruel young boy does who knows no better, torturing innocent animals.

Such extreme mental and emotional pressure was bound to lead to the worm turning, and that happened in March 1979, when a vicious confrontation took place between the father and the two girls. Annette and Charlene were only twenty-one and eighteen respectively at this time, but young as they were, they both decided that the bully would have to be challenged or things would be even worse, if that were possible. A terrible fight took place in the room downstairs and then on the stairs, as the girls ran for refuge upstairs. As they struggled on the stairs, Maw and Charlene were locked in a struggle of real desperation and violence, and he was kicked in the face. He fell backwards but still managed to return to the fray, going upstairs and smashing his way into the room where his daughters waited in terror. But then Beryl Maw arrived and she cracked her husband on the skull with a mirror.

At last, there were three abused women who had their tormentor lying prostrate before them, at their mercy. It was a chance to escape the reign of terror for ever. There was a council of war downstairs: murder was an option at that point. But the events of that awful day read like a scene from a Hollywood horror movie, because as they decided to call the police (and to do that Charlene had to go and use a phone next door), the other two women went to check on Maw, and as they approached him, he awoke and grabbed Annette's throat. It was so horrific she thought that he would kill her, and that does seem like a real possibility. The girl gasped that her mother would have to take a knife to the man, and Beryl did. It is hard to imagine how she must have felt in that situation, as she scrambled down to fetch a knife, then she returned and gave it to Charlene, who plunged it into her father's belly. The handle broke off and the man was still choking his daughter, so Beryl brought another blade and this time Charlene was more successful: she stabbed him in the neck and he bled to death.

At Leeds Assizes, the charge was manslaughter, not murder, and that is quite in accord with the situation and with that sequence of events on the night of the killing. Pleas of not guilty to murder were accepted. The daughters were given a three-year sentence and the mother was not charged with any related offence. In terms of the language and concepts of the law, here we are talking about a partial defence to murder, that is, an idea pointing to the notion of the 'slow-burn' reaction more typical of women than men – a slower response of violence to a scene of provocation. The defence that reduces such a homicide to manslaughter is that there has to be a 'sudden loss of control.' It would make no sense to see the Maws' situation as anything but a form of self-defence, as surely the father would have throttled his daughter had he not been stopped. The 'self-control' notion hardly enters into the discussion.

A vigorous campaign began to free the young women. Two Bradford MPs, Thomas Torney and Benjamin Ford, were very active in this, with Torney actually writing to the Lord Chancellor about the case. Other professionals involved in various penal organisations stated that the sentence was unfair and some said, 'excessively severe'. There was a certain amount of sympathy from the forces of law, also. DCS Lapish said to *The Times*, that he had had 'no hesitation in giving them bail' when they were arrested.

The facts were there for all to hear and respond to: here was a monster who had forced the girls to watch as he had gassed mice, bitten off the head of a chicken and kicked a puppy to death. The legal organisation were quoted as saying at the time of the campaign that: 'In numerous manslaughter cases, offenders who have suffered less provocation than the sisters have been given light or non-custodial sentences.'

But in the end, the sentence for Annette was upheld, while that of her sister was reduced by six months.

CHAPTER 22

A Plot to Kill in Sheffield 1989

A ménage à trois *is always a recipe for disaster . . .*

famous writer once said that it was a tough job to give life and not anyone could do it, but anyone who could lift a spade could give death. Death was indeed all too easy to give out in the dark in Crookes Park, Sheffield, in 1989. Three people who had apparently spent a happy night drinking together walked into that park but only two came out, to walk home and into the bed they shared. The woman was Anita Bessant and the man Ian Barnard. The body left in the park, cut into pieces, was that of Anita's husband, David. In one of the most cruel and heart-rending ironies of murder cases, the parents of David Bessant were later to find the birth certificates of their grandchildren in a litter bin among the mess that was the home of the killers.

For some time, stripper Anita had been enjoying an open affair with Ian Barnard, a tearaway biker, and her husband had been able to do nothing about it. David Bessant continued being humiliated and going back home for more. Even after some time away in Bristol, when he ought to have accepted the inevitable, he still came back to Sheffield to suffer more at the hands of his wife and her new partner. Anita had always had other men, and that had driven poor David to depression and even attempted suicide. His wife would have been a handful for anyone: she was well-built and strong, with a magnetic sex appeal. Even though she worked in a rough area, the men were there and so was the raw, exciting lifestyle that she craved.

When Anita met Ian Barnard, there was a meeting of kindred spirits. She changed her name to Barnard by deed-poll and the split seemed permanent. This must have seemed even more

apparent when David met and
lived with another woman. But
that woman told *True Crime
Magazine* in 2004 that David
Bessant had still loved Anita
and longed to be in her company.

The tales of the spurned husband's humiliation take some
believing. Once he was carried
out of the house while asleep by
two men who then took his wife
to bed. Anita's habit of having a
variety of men share the bed even
extended to alternating weeks
with husband, and then her lover.

The woman who styled herself
'The White Witch' because of

'The White Witch'. Laura Carter

her interests in such subjects as tarot cards and in vaguely occult
pursuits, worked her magic on her new man, so much so that
she began to use her powers of persuasion in a direction that
would lead to murder. The reasoning was simple but powerful
and recalls Shakespeare's Lady Macbeth:

> *. . . there is a man in the way of our happiness, and think what
> you would have if he were removed.*

The plan was for the *ménage à trois* to have a night out in the
Sheffield pubs and then attack David on the way home. A
ménage à trois is always a recipe for disaster.

Running through Barnard's mind that night must have been
Anita's words: 'When he is out of the way you can spend every
week in my bed.' Strangely, and in hindsight, with extreme
callousness, the threesome were laughing and happy when they
came out of the last pub of the night. But in the park, Barnard
turned on David and began to attack him with a knife.

Imagining the scene early next morning as people drifted into
the park to walk their dogs or have a quiet jog is a grim effort of
will; something in the mind resists the thought of finding such
slaughter on a normal day when the world is waking up. But
what passers-by saw was a bloody corpse. The man's throat was
slashed open and he was in a pool of his own blood. There were

Crookes Park, c.1930. Author's collection

cuts and slash-marks all over his body. But it was not going to be hard to find the killers unless something drastic happened. After all, the threesome were widely known and there were metaphorical signposts to the two co-habitees of the dead man. Anita was interrogated and she confessed; her mind did not have the strength or resolve to match her physical strength. She admitted that there had been a murder pact and that she was responsible for the germination of the intent to kill.

At the trial in Sheffield, in 1990, everything was clear-cut. Barnard had come clean about his role in the killing, and even more repulsive, it emerged that Anita had earlier warned her husband that her lover was out to kill him, saying: 'Ian has been thinking of doing you over.' What the popular press developed into a racy and sensational notion of the woman choosing her sexual partner with the flip of a coin did not quite match what she herself said in court: 'I said if I had to choose one of them, I would have to flip a coin because my emotions were not stable enough for me to make that decision.' The picture that emerged reflected the Lady Macbeth motive once again; because Barnard changed his plea to guilty, his most promising move in the repertoire of defence was to stress that he had been egged on, as was Macbeth, to do the deed.

The picture painted was that Anita worked on her lover's mind to such a degree that he developed a wild and irrational detestation of David Bessant. On the night of the killing, he was seen by several people to be in a tense and nervous state. Maybe the pressure was too much, the mind games too extreme, and one option lay open to him if he were to be free of the 'problem' as David Bessant then was seen to be.

The judge certainly saw the situation as one in which the woman at the centre of all this had exerted terrible pressure and had broached the idea of murder (in court she had tried to say that this had been 'a joke' but that soon wore thin). She was sentenced to life imprisonment and the judge said: 'You are a selfish, wilful and wicked woman who must now suffer the consequences of your conviction for murder.'

This case is arguably a template for all those stories of deadly relationships in which power games, driven by sexual possession and dependence, lead to the most destructive emotions. In the long line of murders committed by or involving women, this is highly unusual, however. The internal web of violent feelings was such that a victim suffered entrapment, being led on to believe that he was welcome in the sick threesome in which the woman at the heart of it was and surely always would be the object of his desires.

The first reports of the case created a media frenzy of the ridiculous tag of 'White Witch' attached to the woman in question. In fact, beneath all that hype, there was merely a rather pathetic obsession. Although at the centre of this case is a murder pact, it is still in some ways atypical of that phenomenon. If we were to concoct any kind of label for this highly irregular murder, it would surely be a 'Lady Macbeth' homicide. That is, the urgings and plottings leading to the horrendous death of a loving and trusting man were from a sick source: a dark current of hatred and possession flowing from the cruel desires of someone who knew nothing of love and too much about relentless and murderous sexual desire.

The 'White Witch' profile had no real substance. It simply referred to dabblings and whimsical interests in subjects that had nothing to do with the sorcery we associate with the medieval cases of witchcraft. It was, finally, in spite of the popular press, an example of a kind of subterfuge, something covering the base and squalid intentions inside that black heart. But murder sells papers and improves television audience ratings, and this case was a perfect example of how something essentially mundane and repulsive became a temporary sensation.

Part 3
Curiosities

CHAPTER 23

The Mysterious Murdering Mylneburnes

They feloniously waylaid and murdered Christopher Tinker ...

s commuters drive out of Huddersfield, through Lepton and past Flockton and Emley, they would have no idea, unless they enjoyed digging out records of misdeeds from the violent Tudor years, that they are driving close to a spot where a husband and wife waited for their victim, ready to take his life.

Unfortunately, the account of the murder is known only in fragments, but the basis of the story is that at what was then called Whitcross, near Emley, in 1569, Henry Mylneburne and his wife Elizabeth had some reason to kill Christopher Tinker. The legal language of the case makes it clear that they had malice against him in their minds and they had 'disturbed the peace of the realm' in killing him.

The phrase 'malice aforethought' but in its Renaissance English, is written in the court rolls. They also had help from another Mylneburne, and it may be that there was a clan-like vendetta at work here. Whatever the reason, Elizabeth Mylne-burne joined in and the poor victim was shot and he was blinded in the left eye, before being tortured. What had he done to merit such horrendous treatment from this gang of mur-derous Mylneburnes? That we will never know, but we do know that the family were not part of the murderous underclass or of the travelling thieves that plagued Tudor England. Henry was 'a yeoman' born in 'Whitcrosse' and still living there at this time. Some evidence must have led the investigation to feel that he had a background of wilful hatred towards his victim, and so had Elizabeth. The couple were in fact supposed to have 'dia-bolical' motives for what they did. It is the kind of case that leads us to speculate, as the facts are so threadbare. All we can say it that it was a very insecure system of law at that time in the rural areas of England. Law had to cope with almost tribal violence at times, as families exercised the right of revenge. The family was the basis of protection, and this Emley case has all the hallmarks of a family affair. The idea of an 'investigation' is a slender concept, as the reality was that someone would merely come forward with a recognizance, a statement that they considered a person to have done a felonious act to break the Queen's peace.

The most likely scenario is that the Mylneburnes had a very personal reason to ambush and kill their man. Throughout Elizabeth I's reign, there were continual attempts to legislate away the troublesome northern counties. In fact, this murder happened in the same year as the rising in the north, a rebellion that forced the Queen to raise an army of 28,000 men. So both on a grand scale and at a local level, murders were a common way of settling disputes, and the isolated villages around the West Riding were confident that they could sort out family arguments and regional confrontations by force of arms. What happened to these three killers, Elizabeth among them, we do not know for sure.

As they had a certain amount of local status and social presence, in spite of the act being a felony, they may have escaped with a large fine. In the worst cases, one of the felons would have taken the main blame and then disappeared into another parish, suffering a kind of banishment.

The curiosity in this killing is that it is teeming with unanswered questions. But it is one small narrative in the story of Emley and Elizabeth Mylnebyrne was quite happy to pick up a weapon and batter the victim she and her husband wanted out of the way.

CHAPTER 24

They Escaped the Noose
Long Riston, 1799

... they did beat, wound and ill-treat him so that of his life it was greatly despaired ...

Beverley in the last years of the eighteenth century was trying to keep up with its grand neighbour, York, and other country towns with a dash of culture and gentry. In fact, throughout the eighteenth century, the planning and architectural development had been impressive. The rebuilding of the town hall came in 1762, and the courthouse and other municipal buildings were to enhance the appearance of this attractive market town, a place of social meetings, hostelries, and visitors on their way to the coast. But beneath this lay the usual dark problems and violence of the Georgian years.

In the last year of the eighteenth century, when the so-called Age of Reason was flowering, the East Riding Assizes were to witness one of the most repulsive and inhuman cases the annals of murder have ever recorded. It happened at the village of Long Riston, a place described in the nineteenth century as:

> ... *standing on the high road from Hull to Breverley, eleven miles from the former place and nineteen from the latter ... There are chapels in the village belonging to the primitive and Wesleyan Methodists erected in 1836. The National School was built by subscription for the accommodation of 100 Children ... It is endowed with about £12 per annum, left by Peter Nevill in 1807.*

Around the turn of the century, just as religion and local philanthropy were having an effect, there was one little boy who would not be attending that new national school. His name was Thomas Hostler.

At the midsummer assizes for 1799 the true nature of the cruel death of little Thomas was recorded for posterity in the careful and ornate longhand of 'B. Ford.'

What happened was that the boy's father, William, together with his wife Jane and his sister-in-law, Elisabeth Beal, who had all been maltreating little Thomas, went too far. Neighbours could take it no more; they had witnessed extreme cruelty and this had been happening over a long period. Finally, they acted.

Four people of the village took out a recognizance against the three abusers, and at that time the child was still alive. Christopher Hall, Elisabeth Chadwell, Sarah Wray and Mary Ford stated upon oath that the three defendants had physically abused the little boy, most intensively, over a period of several

Beverley Sessions House. Author's collection

Assize record for the Hostler case. East Ridings Archives

weeks in June of that year. That document meant that each of the accusers was bound to pay £30 to his majesty George III if the action failed. There was going to be little chance of that ever happening. What had been done to the boy was savage beyond belief.

This was not a case of what some medical historians write of as 'neonaticide'. This was a toddler, in modern language, and what the evil trio was accused of was expressed in the assize records in this way:

> ... *with their hands and feet and with whips and staves and sticks they did strike and kick, beat and whip over the head and neck and shoulders, back, belly, sides and posteriors, feet and other parts of the naked body of him the said Thomas Hostler in a*

A recognizance for a murder accusation. East Riding Archives

cruel and inhuman manner, giving him by such strikes, beatings and whippings, large and grievous wounds, swellings and bruises on the right side of his head about the temples and several large stripes on his neck.

These assaults, repeatedly administered over the weeks in question and probably before people began to take notice, were vicious but also almost systematically done, to affect every part of the child's body as if there was an intention to inflict pain and wounds in a certain manner with predesigned effects.

The records make a special mention of the two women involved – Elisabeth Beal and the mother, Jane: 'Jane his wife and Beal did other wrongs to the said Thomas Hostler then and there, did to the great damage of Thomas Hostler and against the peace of the said Lord ... did beat, wound and ill-treat so that of his life it was greatly despaired ...'

There was special mention of what Jane did between 2 February and 10 April, noting that she savagely battered the child so that he was near death. The accounts and language used there suggest that there was a sadistic pleasure here, a twisted kind of satisfaction in inflicting harm on the little boy. But their time was up, and the law had tracked them down. The boy does appear to have been dead at the time that the jury came to a decision. This was not expressed in the record, though we know from a separate second action against the trio that he was dead. At the assizes, the foreman of the jury signed the record, along with the witnesses, Will Iveson, Francis Jackson, Mary Ford, Sarah Wray, Elisabeth Maxwell and Christopher Hobbs.

The document, however, hints at another mystery and at another story, because initially the word 'Guilty' was written after the names of all three, but then the word 'Guilty' after William Hostler's name was lined through. 'Not Guilty' was written after that.

We must assume that the child died just before the proceedings took place, though this is not openly stated. However, in a second recognizance, one John Dawson of Beverley swore that he would appear before the next general sessions 'to proffer a bill of indictment against William Hostler, wife and Beal.' On that document the sentence is added: 'For the murder of the infant Thomas.' The date of this document is 1 June, so the child must have died just before that.

But what of the strange tale of why William Hostler was acquitted. Why was the word 'guilty' expunged from the record and why was he released? We have to speculate on the reasons for this. Perhaps there was another narrative beyond this one, something relating to family morality or to the fact that at one point

The felon in the stocks. Laura Carter (based on an old print)

The pillory as shown in The Newgate Calendar. Clifford Elmer

the man was trying to take the blame for his wife. But this seems unlikely, given that several people appear to have had a close knowledge of what was going on in the Hostler household. Cynically, we might wonder if he had friends in high places. Whatever the reason, there is a tantalising untold story behind the crossing-out of the word 'Guilty'. The simple but obvious answer might just be that he was the head of a household and that some local people thought that he should remain so that the estate and property (and his work) could keep on. But in the second recognizance he is named, by John Dawson. Two conditions of recognizance named him.

The two women were in for a hard time: they were to be pilloried, then sent to York Castle and from there transported. The pillory had been only recently maintained in Beverley, and this punishment was often combined with whippings, as illustrations from the period make clear. Not until an act of 1837 was the pillory abolished. Stocks and pillories were widespread at the time of this murder, though. There were over 11,000 pillories in England in 1700.

With a terrible local crime such as this, repugnant to all the sound family values on which the community was based, there was a call for humiliation as well as for the villains to disappear into York, out of sight and mind. Whippings in public were a related punishment, and such was the fate of Thomas Roberts

Beverley Magistrates' Court today. The author

The Beverley the Hostlers would have known. The author

of Beverley, who was whipped in 1822 for stealing two pairs of women's shoes.

Jane and Elisabeth were to spend some time in the dark hovels within York Castle and then be shunted onto a cart, taken to a ship and given the tough experience of a journey to Van Dieman's Land. Statistics at that time would have been against their survival.

CHAPTER 25

Letting Go Was Too Hard
Bridlington, 1909

*Her precarious state of health in the
dock made high drama.*

There are some stories from the lives of young women who led precarious and uncertain lives in service, or drifting from job to job across Yorkshire, that create interest because they throw light on the kind of human dilemmas that never go away. Some of these stories are tragic on a grand scale, whereas others are of a lower order, seedy and mundane. But there are also some of these tales that exist mainly as morality tales about the fallibility of human nature. Into this category falls the life of Maud Waines.

In August 1909, the *Bridlington Gazette* announced that in the local magistrates' court there had been something very much out of the ordinary run of things in this sleepy seaside town: 'There are many details which are not fit for publication and it is only necessary to refer to the Chairman's suggestion that all respectable women, and respectable men too, should go out of the court, to indicate the nature of the case.' This brings to mind the famous saying about the British public by Lord Macaulay: 'We know of no spectacle so ridiculous as the British public in one of its periodical fits of morality.' One would have thought that the *Gazette* was trying to protect the sensibilities of a weak and gullible public.

What in fact was happening was that Maud Waines, a frail-looking girl of twenty-two who looked much younger, was in the dock on what was looking like a murder trial. It had all begun when one morning in July a man called Stubbs, as he was walking on Sands Lane railway bridge in Bridlington, found a parcel containing the body of a baby wrapped in linen. Good police work had tracked down the laundry numbers on the linen to the home of a Mrs Crannis at 2 Marlborough Terrace in the town. It has to be said that the detective involved, Robson, did excellent work using the laundry numbers on towels and aprons. This required close observation and attention to detail. What it did most of all was lead to Maud Waine, who was living in St John Street.

So began our knowledge of this sad, lonely young woman, who had been led to a desperate act by her 'downfall', as seduction was expressed then. The indications for her future in the legal process were not good when it was noted that the police took possessions away from her. These included a bottle of 'apioline', a substance of some importance later on. A Dr Forrest had examined the corpse of the infant and concluded that it had lived for some little time independently of the mother, so it was not a case of a stillbirth. He noticed a wound on its skull but this seemed to have been caused during the birth. Now he had to care for the mother in court, because Waine was constantly in poor health. She was of a weak constitution and needed attention all the time, as the stresses of the proceedings were hard for her to bear.

Dr Forrest was called to her and she was always escorted, such was the concern. But despite all this, she stood in court

Bridlington, Royal Prince's Parade. Author's collection

Monument Bridge, Hull, where Maud saw her seducer. Author's collection

and faced a charge of wilful murder. She pleaded not guilty and there was an adjournment. On remand, she had the care of the prison doctor in Hull, and he of course was expected to make a report on her. Her lawyer, Mr Wray, had to make announcements on her delicate health and it became clear at the court when she next appeared that she had been more seriously ill in custody. Yet again the case was adjourned. This was guaranteed to interest the local press, as the murder charge combined with the fascination of the woman's condition and frail presence in the dock, made this a good dramatic story.

APIOL AND STEEL PILLS

FOR FEMALES.

A French remedy for all IRREGULARITIES and OBSTRUCTIONS, superseding bitter Apple, Pil Cochiac, Pennyroyal, &c.

PRICE 4/6 POST FREE.

OBTAINABLE ONLY FROM

MARTIN, Foreign Chemist, SOUTHAMPTON.

THE GREAT BLOOD PURIFIER.

THOMPSON'S BURDOCK PILLS.

For purifying the foulest Blood, and removing every Disease of the Stomach, Liver and Kidneys. Cures Scurvy and Scrofula, Sores, Eruptions of the Skin, and all diseases arising from an impure state of the Blood. Gouty and Rheumatic persons will find the greatest relief by their use.

The continued use of these Pills Purifies the Blood, and gives tone and energy to the system. They are especially recommended to seafaring men for quickly removing Salt Water Boils, and to those suffering from the effects of Bad Water, Salt Provisions, &c.

Sold by all Chemists, in Boxes, at 1s. 1¼d. and 2s. 9d. each or by post direct from the Proprietor,

J. THOMPSON, Burdock Pill Manufactory,

44, OXFORD STREET, SWANSEA. For 15 or 34 stamps.

Thompson's ELECTRIC LIFE DROPS for the Cure of Nervous Debility. The Electric Life Drops acts so quickly on a weak and shattered constitution that health is speedily restored. In Bottles, at 5s. 6d., 11s. and £1 2s.; In Cases, at £5.

An advert for the apiol pills, as found in Maud's room. Author's collection

At last, the case was heard and her story was told. Waine had been in touch with a Hull man called Arnold Fisher and he had fixed a visit and a date with her while she was working in Beverley. But the *Gazette* reporter was in for a treat, when the detective Robson, recounted a strange incident. He had been in a cab with Waine in Hull and as the cab stopped on Monument Bridge, the young woman had shrieked and pointed at a man passing by, saying it was Foster, and that he was the father of the dead child. She even knew that he worked at the Hull firm, British Oil Mill Company.

It was then that the sad story emerged. Waine had been working in service, moving from post to post, and had met Foster, in search of a little excitement. He had wooed her, courted her and made promises, of course. But she had been seduced and became pregnant. Luckily, she had a friend and support in a woman called Louise Botterill in Bridlington, and she took care of the little child for the first six weeks until Waine found a position elsewhere. The long tale of misfortune grad-

The centre of Hull as it would have been in Maud's time. Author's collection

ually emerged. Waine had had the child, moved jobs and then returned to Bridlington. There was no definite detail about the child and when and where she was seen with him around the date of the finding of the body. What was confirmed, though, was the medical evidence stating that the death had been due to a fall.

Waine had previously been sacked from one place of employment due to her illness. Again, in the magistrates' court, she fainted. Her precarious state of health in the dock made high drama. Generally, the opinion was forming that she had not killed the child; evidence pointed to her love of children and her good nature. What was coming through as the truth here was that the child had died and she had held on to it for a while. The sympathy for her was now palpable and in court the bench decided that this was not a murder charge. Her lawyer in her defence made a plea for a much lesser charge to be applied. The outcome would be heard at York Assizes.

There, on 17 November, the charge Maud Waine faced was not murder, but merely concealment of birth. The presiding judge, Mr Justice Bucknill, a bencher of the Inner Temple, made it clear that this was not a murder case and said that the truth was that the girl had hidden the body of her child 'recently

A typical series of adverts for quack remedies. Author's collection

Albert Dock, Hull, at the time of the case. Author's collection

born'. The defence lawyer painted a sad picture of the woman giving birth while unconscious, and that the child had had the fall. Most likely, it had survived a few months but died of injuries sustained at the time. There were plenty of good things said about her character, and the most astonishing sidelight we have on her true nature from all this is how tough she was, in spite of ill health, and also that she was driven to desperation by the stigma of illegitimate birth. She had suffered in silence and not told her Burton Agnes family, going alone through the demands of the pregnancy.

The result was a binding over and a fine of £5. We have to point the finger of blame at the man from Hull, as indeed Mr Justice Bucknill did. But there was nothing to be done in that quarter. Overall, the tale of Maud Waine is one of its time: a saga of public shame and inner humiliation, all stemming from a desire to have some fun and break the monotony of life in service.

As for the 'apiolene' Maud had in her room, this was basically parsley extract, used for easing the spasms associated with dysmenorroea, and indeed for supposedly bringing on a miscarriage, as implied by adverts such as that in the *Clock Almanac* for 1906. Apium petroselinum treats 'disturbances connected with utero-ovarian congestion' (Cook's *New Materia Medica,* Chicago).

Almost Murder
Elizabeth Ward, 1816

Her execution was scheduled at York.
She seemed to have nine days left.

Elizabeth Ward was only seventeen when she very nearly killed her sister-in-law. She was destined to hang for it, and in spite of a plea to the judge it was no use, and he would not commute the sentence, despite her youth. He thought she should be an exemplar case to deter others. *The Times* reported it, picking out this aspect: 'One enormous case occurred at York – that of Elizabeth Ward, seventeen years of age, who was convicted of the horrid crime of administering poison to her sister, and is to suffer death.' The paper got the facts slightly wrong, but it picked out the repugnance of the affair.

In July 1816, Elizabeth went from her home in Rothwell into Leeds (only a few miles away) and bought two ounces of arsenic. She was seen the next day mixing white powder into a milk and oatmeal porridge, by her little brother George, whose statements later would be very important. Her sister-in-law Charlotte was the intended victim, and the fact that she noticed something amiss with the food is quite astonishing through modern eyes. Most poison victims were unlikely to do this, of course, as the natural inclination is to eat or drink with ease and with speed. But Charlotte, for some reason, sensed something wrong and she noticed the white substance in the jug. She then locked this in a cupboard and even more impressively forcing herself to be sick to vomit up what tiny traces had gone into her blood. As for Elizabeth, she was seen by little George throwing the rest of the food away.

Sensible Charlotte then went for medical advice and consulted a druggist, Mark Poskitt. He and another chemist tested

A hanging scene, from an old print. Author's collection

vomit and found arsenic traces. The teenager had failed in her quest to kill, but it had been a close-run thing. In most cases, the victim would have swallowed enough to kill or at least to cause long hours of horrible suffering. Elizabeth was charged, naturally. There was a motive, and the girl explained this herself when questioned, saying that after Elizabeth's mother had died a few months before these events, Charlotte had become the centre of power in the home and young Elizabeth did not like that at all. But Charlotte came through the effects of the small amount of poison she had taken and went to the magistrate to give the facts.

Nine-year-old George had to testify against his big sister, and he had plenty to say. This was at York Assizes, just a week after the attempted murder. It is stunning to report that there was no defence lawyer for the girl, and yet five witnesses were called. The teenager was allowed to question these people but as we can imagine, she could not put much of a coherent argument together and could simply protest her innocence. There were three druggists lined up against her, and the one from whom she had bought the arsenic in Leeds recognised her. She was doomed.

One odd aspect of the case, as pointed out by historian Katherine Watson, is that Poskitt had no experience of the kind of pathology required in poisoning cases and said that he had learned all he knew from books only. Watson also notes: 'It is also interesting to note that Sutcliffe (a druggist) lived in York, the seat of the assize court. The fact that Poskitt gave him the sample to test indicates that the apothecary was determined to obtain corroboration of his findings.'

All the girl could say after all this science was lined up against her was, 'I am innocent of the crime.' There were several charges against her. Attempted murder was a capital offence under Lord Ellenborough's Act of 1803; she had given poison in a deadly quantity and although there was no evidence of her intention, there was no defence to say otherwise. But she was sentenced to death, and only then did another story emerge. There may well have been a case of insanity in this, but the judge found no reason to commute the sentence. He could have done, and most murder cases ended in a commutation at that time. But this was to be a case of a reprieve.

Even that process was long and uncertain. The sovereign, George III, was mentally incapacitated and the appeal went to the Home Secretary, Lord Sidmouth, and then to the Prince Regent. There was support for the girl in high places, though, and here there was a Yorkshire lobby, from no less a dignitary than Lord Lascelles. It was he who brought about a postponement of the hanging at first, and then, with more time, the city of York and other groups across the county put together a petition that went to the Prince Regent, who directed a reprieve.

CHAPTER 27

A Miscellany of Modern Murder

The late twentieth century brought with it massive social changes which have given a radical new face to the varieties of homicide, as well as every other kind of crime. In Yorkshire, the expansion of communities with new identities has affected this, of course. The phenomenon of 'honour' killings in the West Yorkshire towns could have featured here but I have chosen to exclude it. But there are other contexts for murder, and such developments as the 'girl gang' and new versions of provocation defences have given the narrative of murders by women a new spin. Yet there are some murder cases which merely retell the classic situations of jealousy and possession.

The case of Yvonne Sleightholme demonstrates this variety of murder based on misguided love and possession. On New Year's Eve 1898, Sleightholme met William Smith, a man who was managing a farm in North Yorkshire. They lived together at the farm for over a year before things changed and, from William's standpoint, the relationship was wearing thin and he wanted it to end. He wanted to end their affair but Yvonne had no desire to go along with this and the strange strategies of reprisal began, first of all with a statement out of the blue that she had leukaemia – a ploy that made him soften and move close to her again. This was surely a sign that she would do anything to keep his affection. Mysteriously, the leukaemia was not mentioned again once she had his company and spent time with him again.

But William was developing a friendship with another woman, Jayne Wilford, and this was to be a challenge to Sleightholme, to say the least. One of the decisive events in this story is that Yvonne became pregnant but lost the child, and through her eyes, when William grew closer to Jayne and the latter moved in after Yvonne moved out, this was intolerable.

After William married Jayne, the real problems with the slighted woman began. Never did a killer have a more ironically suitable name than 'Sleightholme.'

The focus of her revenge was Jayne. There were threatening phone calls and then one day the farm barn was set alight. Nothing was pinned on the obvious suspect, and she had now found a boyfriend, but there was a deep resentment still simmering and smouldering inside her. There was going to be a move, however, from phone calls and threats to something more sinister. When William left the home one day, Yvonne was waiting for her victim. After he left and Jayne was left alone, the extent of Sleightholme's wrath was expressed in a callous murder. She had a rifle, and as her victim opened the door, she fired a bullet in her head. There had been some devious and twisted thinking in the planning of this, because she then made it look like a sexual attack, tearing most of the clothes from the body of her victim.

It would not take a genius to look at Sleightholme as a suspect and forensic investigation of her car brought the necessary evidence. A desperate alibi proved useless: the facts were there to see, in the form of Jayne's blood in her car.

Naturally, many more recent murders have come from the new geography of homicide: the stresses of life in rootless communities and in life in which weapons are a way of life. The modern placing of murder and violent crime can be partly explained in the words of the great sociologist Emile Durkheim, who was interested in the isolation of the individual: 'Reality seems valueless by comparison with the dreams of fevered imaginations; reality is therefore abandoned but so too is possibility abandoned when it in turn becomes reality. A thirst arises for novelties, unfamiliar pleasures, nameless sensations, all of which lose their savour once known.' In other words, as modern society has made relationships and communities more difficult to maintain in a fully human way, the results have been destructive. Some killings have been related to groups, gangs, tribes and other kinds of strong allegiances. A case in point is the story of Avril Gregory at Wombwell in 1992.

After a young man called Scott Beaumont was stabbed to death in Wombwell High Street, it emerged that the young women accused had acted because of his behaviour some time before in Cleethorpes. At the time Gregory was just eighteen and the other girl only sixteen. Gregory told her story to Kate Kray for her book, *Killers*, and the importance of this is that the Gregory case is one from which anyone can learn about the nature of 'gang' mentality and also about how death can result from the most minor of incidents. The tale told by Gregory described an almost tribal, instinctive response to a threat, as the other, younger girl accused had been in fear from supposed gang attacks related to Beaumont. That may or may not be true, but at the time it caused the response – a tragic one – of the use of weapons.

Gregory recalls that the girls gathered and had weapons such as knives and tool handles. She says she was not looking for an argument with Scott but 'to show him that we weren't scared of him'. The other girl had used the knife, but Gregory was implicated of course, and not a minor.

From an historian's point of view, the striking thing about this crime is just how radically different it is from anything in the earlier cases. Some murders by women in recent times have shown similarities with the 'classic' cases, but this story typifies a profound change in the way we live, and of course in the way Yorkshire has changed.

One way to view the extreme contrast between murders or attempted murders past and present is to recall the case of Hannah Whitley who, in 1789, was convicted of poisoning the child of a neighbour. But it is a perplexing case; she put arsenic in the child's food. Intriguingly, there was a note left, suggesting some kind of witchcraft, saying: 'God damn you all for I can come again and I will send the devil to you, by God.' This happened in Hampsthwaite, where Whitley, after seeming to be helpful in baking a pie for her neighbour, Rhodes, actually put some arsenic in the pie-crust. Little five-year-old Joseph Rhodes was killed. This all appears to have stemmed from a neighbourhood dispute in which Rhodes and a man called Horseman were involved. Whitley played her part for Horseman, or so it seems. She was hanged for it.

Comparing the Whitley case with the Gregory one, we have an interesting contrast. Both women were the same age and both in basically family-oriented smallish communities in Yorkshire. But Whitley's was a silent, devious and planned killing; rather amazingly, although Gregory played her part in Scott Beaumont's death, its premeditation was totally different, though in the eyes of the law, there is no difference between (a) taking poison to put in a pie or (b) laying our weapons in readiness for a confrontation. The 'malice aforethought' says it all.

The chronicle of women murderers in Yorkshire contains the tragic and melancholy stories of infanticide done by desperate women in extreme circumstances of duress, and it also covers accounts of deadly jealousy and possession. The changes in the nature and context of murder over the centuries have given a reflection of the changing patterns of life during and after the advent of the Industrial Revolution. These cases from the archives show that though circumstances change and influences will differ, at the heart of the homicide effected involving women, be it murder, manslaughter, infanticide or even 'self-murder' as suicide was once styled, the motives stay the same, within the same narrow range of explanation. Though some killings in these cases have been compared to the state of mind of Lady Macbeth – an urge to kill for aggrandisement or profit – more often the murders have been for survival, peace of mind or sheer perverse satisfaction through jealousy and possession.

Other comparisons of past and present invite some interesting moral speculations. For instance, as a mark of changing perspectives on infanticide, two case from the 1950s involving women are interesting. The first is a story that could be compared with the Long Riston one of 1799. But, unbelievably, this happened in 1957 in Huddersfield. Mr Justice Oliver in Leeds gave Jean Holdsworth seven years for what was described as 'systematic torture for at least one year'. She had thrashed the child with straps, ostensibly because it was dirty in its habits. She had used straps and 'in a most dreadful fashion . . . caused wounds all over its head, neck and limbs'. Holdsworth was pregnant at the time of the trial and that was a factor in the sentencing. What she did was very close to the Long Riston situation. But sixty years ago the judge's words explain the apparent severity of the sentence (at the time) as he said: 'People must be shown that they cannot ill-treat helpless little children like this without incurring a heavy sentence.'

The other case from that time was the instance of Patrick and Beatrice Conroy in Sheffield, who were actually given a death sentence in December 1953. They were given the death sentence and due to hang at Strangeways after their appeal was dismissed in January 1954 (See section IV). Their little victim was found in a sack in a cellar with fourteen stab-wounds. They were guilty of murder and concealment of birth.

Finally, there is the new understanding of the mental wounds and the ensuing incapacitation in the context of male brutality. As with the Maw case, some other murders are completely understandable, and usually they are reduced to manslaughter, as in the sad story of Winifred Newsome of Leeds. Living on the tough Gipton estate in 1962, she was abused by her husband most severely. He at one time broke her jaw and was in the habit of hitting her with a dog chain and sometimes with a frying pan. This man, whom the court defined as 'a bully and a drunkard', met his end when she stabbed him, and the most telling state-ment in the affair is in her words: 'I did not realise what I had done until they told me.' She was not a murderess, but guilty of manslaughter, and the sentence reflected the understandable leniency of the court.

Part 4

Destinations

CHAPTER 28

Prison, Asylum, Noose or Over the Seas

Fundamental to all the case studies in this book is the baseline definition of murder, as put into words by the great scholar, Sir Edward Coke: 'Murder is when a man of sound memory, and of the age of discretion, unlawfully killeth within any courts of the realm any reasonable creature *in rerum natura* under the King's peace, with malice aforethought either expressed by the party or implied by law, so as the party wounded or hurt, die of the wound or hurt within a year and a day after the same.' As the centuries wore on, all kinds of additions and qualifications to this were due to be made, such as distinguishing infanticide, manslaughter and so on, and also in relating grievous bodily harm to murder, in terms of intention. The fundamental concepts of a *mens rea* (a desire to do the act) and an *actus reus* (the act itself aforethought) are at the basis of all this. But as the law changed, what were the destinations of women, in particular, who had fallen foul of the law?

Some were destined to be transported, taken overseas to what is now Tasmania as producers of children for the new colonies; some were given hard labour for life; some were sent to an asylum for the insane and some, naturally, given the harsh laws in former times, were sent to the scaffold. This section summarises and describes some of those destinations, following the changes in these sentences over the centuries. The main spine of this narrative concerns the nature of defences in court, from the various kinds of provocation to the tricky one of insanity.

First, what about accusations? A useful case study from around Beverley serves to illustrate what happened in the early Georgian period, before the more streamlined systems of the nineteenth century. A person could be brought to the attention of the justices of the peace on suspicion and, if enough people testified, a recognizance was made out. For instance, one Margaret Colley was 'bound by recognizance to appear at the next East Riding Assizes on charge of murder.' Two of her own blood were listed in the accusers, who were: 'Thomas Totley, Mary Colley, Mary Corton, Margaret Harper and Sarah Colley.' What she had done was most probably child murder.

On the other hand, some depositions were wild-sounding and irrational, yet still made serious accusations, such as this from 1783, in which a group of people accuse a blacksmith from Etton, Robert Sawdon, of murder, and then they add:

Robert Sawdon being somehow privy to the death of Ann Wilson, late of Etton, and wheareas Elizabeth Wilson, the sister of the deceased, has thrown out several insinuations to confirm this suspicion.

The townsfolk had gone to Francis Best, the justice, with this strange information.

Sometimes, the recognizances accusing murder of a woman are minimal and tell us nothing, as in the accusation put to a woman in 1757: 'William Carnaby, Joseph Maud, John Hall and John Scott have prosecuted Mary Ellah for murder.' That was witnessed by Lord Mansfield.

In the eighteenth century, however, some local cases could be quite expressive of extreme violence, such as this attempted murder case, involving a man and a woman on another woman victim:

Be it remembered on this first day of October, 1768 that Elizabeth Norton of Pocklington, victualler and William Watt, brewer of the same place, came presently before me, one of his Majesty's Justices of the Peace for the East Riding and did acknowledge to our sovereign Lord the King, the said Elizabeth Norton ten pounds and the said Watt five pounds lawful money to be levied on their goods and chattels to the King's use . . . there to answer the complaint of Ann Agar for insulting, assaulting and abusing her lately in Pocklington Street and for frequently instigating, persuading and advising the said husband of the same Ann Agar to leather and even to murder her which he deposed was true . . .

So before the county constabulary and before any kind of national police force was formed, a person could be accused by a group and they could testify according to their beliefs, suppositions and theories. No detection would occur other than a disquisition at the court. Women at that time, therefore, were susceptible to charges of witchcraft or poisoning on little evidence. The way that the early Georgian criminal law worked, as reflected in these documents, makes it plains that a woman on her own, or perhaps a young woman terrified by various terrors associated with birth, would be desperate. In such matters as abortions, for instance, as Susan Steinbach has explained, there would be desperate measures taken in the throes of that fear: 'Medieval abortifacients – pills, herbs or other substances taken by mouth were more common than surgical methods. Traditional medicine offered bleeding, purgatives, emetics and suppositories.' A young woman who took a criminal measure to escape these terrors would be rounded on, reviled, and most likely become the subject of another one of these recognizances.

The woman has been accused then. What are the possible destinations? First of all, the good one – an acquittal.

Acquittal: Leven Carr Poisoning (1871)

In some ways, little changed by 1871 in terms of the problems attached to alleged poisoning. One major Yorkshire case, almost forgotten by historians, took place at that date in Leven Carr.

On 19 May 1871, two bodies were taken from Harper's farm at Leven Carr. They were Matilda Harper, aged fifty, and her granddaughter, Lilly Taylor, only four years old. A nineteen-year-old servant, Hannah Bromby, was arrested and remanded in custody. The general opinion was that the young woman had poisoned the two deceased. Superintendent Wright took the girl away and a widespread scandal rocked the Beverley area.

William Harper, of Linley Hill, had been in Beverley on business and when he came home in the evening he saw that his wife and the little girl were ill. When he asked what was wrong, it was said that the water pump had just been mended and that they were sick after drinking water from the pump. But things were said about a boiling kettle with froth pouring from the lid, and these details, together with mention of red lead apparently being poured into the stream by Bromby, led to Harper walking into the girl's room the morning after the deaths and accusing

The Fatal Poisoning Case at Leven Carr.

CHARGE OF WILFUL MURDER.

On Saturday morning, Superintendent Wright, of the East-Riding Constabulary, applied for a warrant against Hannah Bromby, the under servant at Mr. Harper's, and during the day proceeded to Mr. Harper's residence, and took her into custody. She was taken before Mr. Wylie on Saturday afternoon, charged with the wilful murder of Mrs. Harper and her grandchild, by the administration of arsenic, on the 19th May, and was remanded until Tuesday next. The prisoner, who did not seem at all concerned, is about seventeen years of age, and has been in Mr. Harper's service since Martinmas. The arrest has caused great excitement in Beverley and the neighbourhood.

On Tuesday, at the East Riding Court House, before R. Wylie, Esq., Hannah Bromby, nineteen years of age, was charged with committing murder by poisoning Matilda Harper, aged fifty years, and Lily Marian Taylor, aged four years, at Linley Hill, Leven, near Beverley, on the 18th of May. The prisoner is an inoffensive-looking girl, and during the examination, which lasted over five hours, sat patiently listening to the evidence. The only emotion shown by her was at the close of the inquiry, when she parted with her friends in court.

Mr. Dale, of York, prosecuted, and Mr. Summers defended. Mr. Dale having stated the facts to be proved, called

Mr. William Harper, residing at Linley Hill, in the parish of Leven, who said that on Thursday, the 18th, became to Beverley, and at the time of leaving home his wife and granddaughter were well. He had tea to his breakfast, and felt no ill effects from his breakfast. He returned home soon after eight o'clock in the evening, and saw his wife and granddaughter sat in front of the fire. They complained of being sick, attributing their illness to water from the pump, which had been repaired. They afterwards went to bed; remaining there until they died. Saw Hannah Bromby about five o'clock in the morning of Saturday, the 20th, in her bed-room. Her mother was with her. He said to the prisoner, "I believe you have murdered both my wife and child," and she never spoke a word. At that time she was in bed. He had said nothing to her since.—By the Court: The kettle is not a copper one.—By Mr. Summers: The girl professed to be ill, and her mother had been sent for in consequence.

Mary Anna Harper, only surviving daughter of the last witness, said that when tea was being prepared on the 18th, she noticed something slate-coloured boiling out of the kettle lid, and she told prisoner to empty the kettle and re-fill it from the river, and prisoner went out to do so. Afterwards Mrs. Harper put some water from the kettle into the teapot, and witness put the tea in. Her mother, her niece (four years old that day), and herself partook of tea. They had pork, bread, and custard. Her niece had a mug half full of tea and milk. Witness had partaken of the same pork and bread before that day, but had felt no ill effects from it. At tea her niece complained of being ill, and Mrs. Harper gave her a drink of tea from her cup. She almost immediately vomited, and did so several times after leaving the house. About ten minutes afterwards Mrs. Harper complained, remarking that she thought the water must be greasy, it burnt her mouth like pepper. In the garden, about ten minutes afterwards, she vomited several times. Witness was also sick and had headache. She left about half of her tea in her cup, and her mother only took about two or three tablespoonfuls of tea. The servant, Ash, said she emptied the teapot after tea. A bricklayer, named Henry Dunn, had some tea about five minutes after witness and others had had tea. The only thing he had in common with themselves was tea; he might, perhaps, have bread. Believed he complained of sickness. Dr. Calvert arrived about nine o'clock that evening, and he gave witness, her mother, and niece some medicine. About six ducks died on the Thursday at tea time. Bromby had emptied some red-lead at the grate, and some of us said the ducks had been to the grate. During the morning her mother and the prisoner had had some words. In consequence of what the servant Ash said to witness, she said to Bromby, "I shall not have my mother insulted by you." Bromby made no reply, and witness told her she should leave at once. The prisoner entered witness's father's employ last January. Mrs. Harper and the prisoner had some words about a week before the poisoning took place; it was about milking some cows. — By the Court: Was not aware of any arsenic being kept on the premises. There was cream on the tea table. — By Mr. Summers: When witness told Bromby to empty the kettle she was three or four yards away from her. The sink or drain was six or seven yards from the back door. Saw the red-lead in the grate, but it was not of the colour of the stuff coming from the kettle.

Dr. Calvert, of Brandesburton, stated that in conse-

pleaded guilty and was committed to prison for three months.——Annie Selcombe, Faith Cammell, Jane Boddy, Harriett Lenadon, Martha Blakeley, and Ellen Timpson were summoned by P.C. Kirkman for wheeling perambulators on the footpath in Whitefriargate.—They all pleaded guilty, and were cautioned and ordered to pay the costs.

THURSDAY.—Henry Ferguson, brought up on remand charged with stealing two fowls, the property of Mr. J. Duncan, Anlaby-road, was again remanded eight days.——Ellen O'Donnell, a girl, who has been several times remanded on a charge of stealing linen from another little girl named Ann Foster, was ordered to be imprisoned for seven days, and afterwards to be sent to the Howard Hill Reformatory, Sheffield, for five years.——Anne Boyd, a young woman, was charged by P.C. Tidd (126) with being drunk and disorderly in Bridge-street.—Fined 1s. and costs. —— A man named John Mc.Nally was charged with resisting Police-constable Tidd (126) by attempting to rescue the prisoner Boyd from his custody. Fined 5s. and costs.——Peter Hennigan was brought up on remand charged with stealing two half sovereigns from a boy named Edward Rogan. The boy was sent by a married sister to get a Post-office order for £1 cashed. The money was wrapped up in paper, and whilst loitering in West-street he dropped it out of his waistcoat pocket. Prisoner was seen to deliberately go to the place and pick up the money and walk away without making any inquiries as to who had lost it.—Prisoner now pleaded guilty, and was committed to prison for two months.

Hull News *report of the Leven Carr case, 1871.* Hull News

the servant of murder. He said simply: 'I believe you have murdered both my wife and child.'

He was convinced that arsenic had been used, although organs had only just been taken away for examination by the local doctors. Mary, his daughter, spoke at the first inquest at the police court in Beverley, saying that when tea was being prepared on the fateful day, she noticed something slate-coloured boiling out of the kettle lid. Everyone had a meal consisting of pork, bread and custard. Two days before, some ducks had died at the grate by the pump, and it was noted that the red lead had been dumped then, by Bromby. Now, as various other witnesses spoke, the line of thought was that all had only one substance in common in what they had consumed that evening: the tea. As Bromby had made the tea, the finger pointed at her. What Hannah had said on being arrested was, simply: 'Well, I have never seen any of the stuff since I came into the house. I filled the kettle from the pump, and I cannot say any more.'

The situation was, then, that Harper had made the accusation on no evidence but merely on a gross assumption. Unfortunately, he was in the position of power and Hannah was merely the under-servant. What was needed then was some kind of medical evidence.

Dr Calvert of Brandesburton spoke, saying that labourer Henry Dunn, who had joined in the tea-drinking and the meal, was ill and needed treatment. He had vomited, had stomach pains, burning in the throat, great thirst and drowsiness. The assumption had been made, in an age when arsenic misuse was common, that he had been poisoned, as had the two dead members of the family. Other tests revealed that there was arsenic in the water that had been in the kettle, and the organs taken for study revealed these features, as described in the report written by Dr William Proctor:

> *I have had considerable experience in cases of poisoning. The first liver in jar one contained a stomach and a portion of a small intestine, which showed arsenic in larger quantities than the liver. The condition of the stomach was quite consistent with the condition expected from arsenical poisoning.*

But in the pumped water he found nothing other than what would be expected in terms of organic matter. Arsenic was also found in vomit taken from a grass sod on which Mrs Harper had first been sick.

Everything seemed to point to arsenic being placed in the kettle, and a detail suggests that the young girl had been asked to fill the kettle from the stream, not from the pump, after the white furry substance had gathered on the lid. It seems likely that there was arsenic in the water from the stream, but that is hard to imagine.

The result was that there was no evidence at all to implicate Bromby. The *Hull News* reported on the outcome in this way:

> *Mr Wylie said that he intended following the instructions con-*
> *tained in the 25 section of the 11th and 12th Victoria chap. 24.*
> *He was of the opinion that the evidence given on the part of the*
> *prosecution was not such as to raise a strong and probable pre-*
> *sumption as to the guilt of the accused, and he therefore dismissed*
> *the case. If more evidence could be obtained further proceedings*
> *might be instituted and the depositions now taken would be*
> *available should any of the witnesses die in the interval. Bromby*
> *then left the court, a slight attempt at applause being immediately*
> *suppressed.*

What we have then is a case in which hugely misguided assumptions were made simply because such poisonings were so common; but to charge wilful murder when there were so many other variables having a bearing on the case was wrong-headed in the extreme. To add to our sympathy for Hannah Bromby, we also learn from the local paper that Hannah herself had been seen being sick, by a labourer, James Toughey. She was genuinely ill. That more than any other detail, helped the court to see that she was not the culprit.

Was there a culprit? Arsenic exists naturally in soil, fish and molluscs. We have to ask whether there was more than a normal concentration of arsenic in the organic matter around the stream-water that day.

Transportation

The two women convicted of the 1799 child murder in Long Riston would have been pilloried, sent to York Castle, and then put on board a hulk (a prison ship) in the Thames estuary before sailing for Australia. The first fleet to Botany Bay left in

1786 and transportation continued until 1868. The women on these ships had a very hard time, of course. When the very first fleet left England there were eleven ships and there were 586 males and 191 females on board. As historians have shown, the women were hard to control and prostitution was rife. Sometimes the women were put in irons for this practice, as aboard the *Lady Penrhyn* in 1787.

A typical case would be like that of Charlotte Barnacle, who was convicted of murder, along with her friend. They had put arsenic in the tea of their employer, not intending to kill her but to make a suffer a little. Clearly they were very wrong. But the jury were lenient, and although the judge was sure that they had intended a malicious act, it was agreed that they were not guilty of 'intending to take away life'.

She arrived in Hobart in 1843, and there she married and had a child. But she and her husband absconded and began a new life in mainland Australia, where they were involved in the mining industry in Tarrawingee. She died in 1896, aged seventy-three.

During the journey, Charlotte would have worn clothes of flannel. In 1849, Alexander Kilroy was campaigning for women convicts to be given thicker and stronger shoes, because he reckoned their thin old shoes were a cause of catarrhal illness. There was no clothing available for the children who came on

Sketch made from a print about prison ships. Laura Carter

Where they ended up – Van Dieman's Land Gaol. The author

board; they were in rags from start to finish. Later, the Quaker, Elizabeth Fry had an impact on conditions for women on the ships; she formed ladies' committees and this meant that each individual made a parcel of gifts to give to each female convict before her ship left port. This parcel contained a hessian apron

Port Arthur, Tasmania, entrance to the asylum. The author

and a black cloth one, with a cotton cap and a hessian bag. By 1842 women were being given white jackets and checked aprons in their rations.

Provisions were not so bad. Female prisoners had tea and sugar, and later there was preserved meat and potatoes. But the quantities were not great; in 1844 a man called Clarke tried to increase the ration of one pound of meat for the whole voyage. But there were four sit-down meals a week on some ships, and the fare included pork, plum pudding and gruel.

Deaths on the voyages were still high. On six ships sailing between 1792 and 1794, five women from two hundred died. One problem was the status and nature of the naval surgeon. As Charles Bateson has written:

> As with the naval agent, no attempt was made to define the naval surgeon's powers or to invest him with the requisite authority . . . His lowly position increased his difficulties with the commissioned officers in command of the guard and with masters.

Their journals often give us insights into what women had to endure, as in this instance of a punishment: 'In all the course of my life I never heard such expressions come from the mouth of a human being. The woman's hands were tied behind her back and she was gagged.' The woman in question, Elizabeth Barber, had her hands tied behind her back and was gagged,

A surgeon would look after the women in transit. Author's collection

and she was left like that through the night. Several women were ironed on this particular trip. The journal says: 'The damned whores the moment that they got below, fell a-fighting amongst one another.'

But aboard a ship called the *Friendship* it was very different. There, the women did the washing and mending for the officers. One officer noted that they were perfectly behaved for the whole voyage.

But generally, if the murderer's destination was a convict ship, then they had escaped the noose and if they could survive the journey, they would have a chance of a decent life. They could be given a ticket of leave after five years of good behaviour, which meant that they could go into domestic service or farm work outside the prison colony.

The Asylum

What about the woman who had killed but who was classified as insane? In the years up to the mid-nineteenth century, the asylums could be horrendous, as the basic treatment was forcible restraint and violent suppression of any behaviour deemed unacceptable. Of course, if a person was 'criminally insane' then there was the added perspective of staff not seeing any value in giving them kindness or consideration. It was as late as 1808 that there was any legislation allowing public funds to go into asylums, and it was in 1845 that provision of county asylums was made mandatory.

In York there was a scandal in 1813 after a public inquiry into the asylum there. Yorkshire women who had killed ended up in that asylum when they escaped the scaffold, and their time there was not good at all. The management were dismissed in that year and new staff were brought in. Luckily for York, the new manager was Dr Matthew Allen, the doctor who was later to find fame as the physician who cared for the poet John Clare at High Beech in Epping. Allen was a Yorkshireman and had wandered a little before taking this post, but there, he qualified as a doctor and made the place more humane and open-minded in attitudes.

Asylums were regulated by local boards and there was a system of licensing and of inspection, as the Victorian period wore on. A murderer sent to a Yorkshire asylum would have still been retrained but there would be hot and cold baths and supervision. There were abuses in the early years, with some asylums using whips on patients. But they could also be very humane places and aware of such things as self-harm and suicide risk. For the general public, an asylum still meant 'Bedlam', with all that represented. Public asylums could be made on a very large scale, as in Colney Hatch in London, a place with over 3,000 patients. For some, the tendency in the nineteenth century was for County and Borough asylums to become merely custodial institutions, and arguably this was caused by legislation of 1874, which transferred some of the costs of running the asylums to central funding.

In spite of the rise of psychiatry and the emergence of professional medical staff who specialised in mental health care, even in the early to mid-twentieth century, a case in court in which a murder trial hinged on a defence of insanity often caused major problems, as in those cases such as Louie Calvert in which different experts said different things.

Gaol and House of Correction

Those killers who escaped execution and who were not transported would, naturally, be in prison for life and would have, at times, penal servitude put on them. Until the end of the nineteenth century, this meant the prison life of the treadmill and the cell screw – the demands of turning a wheel in the cell for a specified number of times each day, and the mechanism would be tightened by the 'screw' – the warden.

Wakefield Gaol had a fearsome reputation, as in these words from a song of about 1850:

Such clinking of clogs and shaking of keys,
Croaking of bellies and shaking of knees,
Cursing of beds as hard as a nail.
It would starve the Devil in Wakefield gaol.

The Bradford writer James Burnley visited Wakefield House of Correction in 1874, and this was his impression:

The long lines of whitewashed cells, tier above tier, look as lonely and forsaken as it is possible for habitations to look. They give me a complete idea of a peopled solitude. The seclusion of the hermit, the loneliness of the wilderness, the isolation of the convent can surely not be so oppressive and wearisome as this.

In 1873, 1,825 women were admitted to Wakefield. No women were executed, the total number of executions being only ten, the last one in 1915.

Armley Prison, Leeds, where Louie Calvert was hanged, was built in 1847. As the plans for the design of the grounds and buildings show, there was a wing for female prisoners, one for juveniles and separate exercise yards for the women.

Elizabeth Fry in Newgate: from an 1860 magazine. Author's collection

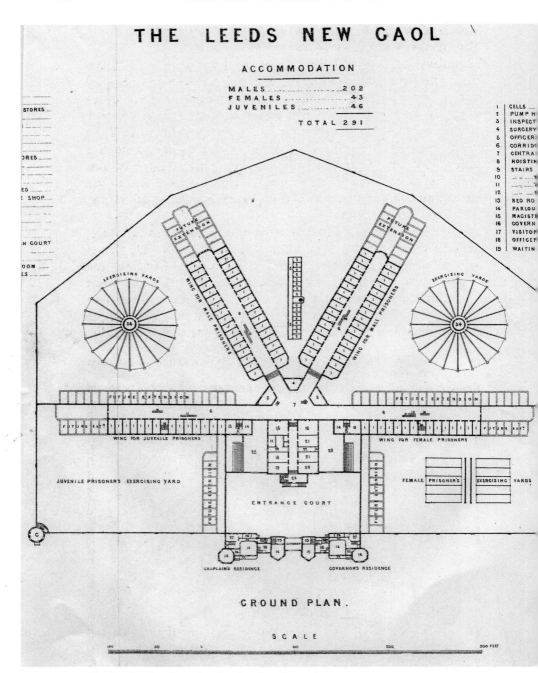

Armley Gaol – plans showing female prisoners' quarters. Author's collection

Mercy Killings: Kathleen Mumford (1938) and
May Brownhill (1935)

There have been several major cases involving women who have killed their own children or other relatives, of course, but by way of 'mercy'. These are clearly very sad and in some cases tragic. In 1938 there had been a case in Newcastle in which a mother cut the throat of her twenty-six-year-old son while he was sleeping. Her reason was that she 'did not want to see him suffer' as he had spinal disease and there was no hope of him living for much longer. She wanted to ease his pain. But it was attempted murder. He survived and gave evidence, describing her as 'a loving parent'.

In the same year in Leeds we have perhaps the most heart-rending murder story ever told. The headline in *The Times* read 'Murder of Imbecile Son' and Kathleen Mumford was sentenced to death. This was on 26 March 1938. Kathleen Mumford had carried her five-year-old son more than fives miles, twice a day over a period of several weeks, in attempts to find treatment for him in clinics and welfare centres. Finally,

Cartoon from The Idler *(1890), hinting at a certain weakness in the judiciary.*
Author's collection

seeing no other option, she placed his head in a gas oven and killed him. Derek was an imbecile and she had stressed when interviewed that there was no hope of any recovery or change for him. 'I have no regrets for what I have done,' she told the press. She went on: 'There was no cure whatsoever for the child. He would never be normal with his hands, therefore what was the child to live for? All the days of his life he would have been an imbecile. Was it right that a child should have to live like that? Therefore, I ended his sufferings.'

But Mr Justice Wrottesley, in his summing up, had to say that there was nothing in law that could justify her taking her son's life: it was murder. The jury found her guilty of wilful murder but with 'the very strongest recommendation to mercy'.

Earlier, Kathleen had been granted bail by Mr Marshall, the magistrate in Leeds. Her story came out then, as the facts of her mercy killing became known. She was forty years old and lived in Middleton, south Leeds, with her husband and their son, Derek. They also had a lodger, as was common practice then. Kathleen had been told that Derek would have to go to a mental home; he had Little's Disease (cerebral palsy) and was an imbecile, so there was no doubt that he would always be incapable of managing his own affairs. She actually asked her GP if she could 'do away with the boy' and, of course, he said that was not an option.

When other health professionals contacted her (after the doctor's anxieties on her behalf), there was a suggestion that the boy be sent to what was then known as a 'mental colony' but Kathleen thought the best plan was for her to move house nearer to Leeds so that he could attend a special school. When she went to Leeds Public Dispensary, it was clear that she was under extreme pressure. She told staff there that she had been unable to sleep and was very depressed. A health visitor shortly after came to the home and saw the child looking pale and ill, just lying on a couch. At that point, Kathleen admitted that she had given him some tablets. These were luminal, and she had given him sixteen tablets. But he lived for more than a day after taking these – his mother gassed him. Kathleen Mumford, in despair, gassed him and then walked to Leeds Town Hall, carrying his body wrapped in cloth.

'I want to give myself up. I have gassed him!' she said. Staff tried to resuscitate the boy but she screamed: 'Don't try to bring him round, he's an imbecile. I have done it with the gas fire. I knelt on the bed and held a tube to him until he went.' He died in Leeds Infirmary.

Kathleen Mumford spent just two days in Aylesbury Prison. There was a decision from the Home Secretary for a pardon.

May Brownhill from Burn Bridge near Harrogate, was in a similar situation. She had given her son 100 aspirin tablets, fearing to leave him to the mercy of others when she herself would be incapacitated. It was a scenario of horrendous emotional turmoil. May Brownhill was sixty-two when she did this; her son was an imbecile, and like Mumford, she gassed him. When she found out that she had to have a major operation and that the chances of her caring for Denis, her thirty-year-old son, were slim, she made the drastic decision to end his life.

On 15 September 1935 she had a particularly bad night of it, and when she retired to bed with Denis, she decided to give him the aspirins and place a gas tube in his mouth.

After her arrest and imprisonment, she had the operation, being taken to the Royal Hospital in Salford for that treatment. As *The Times* reported: 'It commanded the pity of all, but it was no answer to the charge to say that life had been taken from love. Doctors had no right to take life . . . It was not for a parent – even a mother – to judge . . .'. For her defence, May Brownhill had the famous Lord Birkett, and he said, talking to the jury, that the son's life had been 'a veritable living death' and that the crux of the matter was the operation on Mrs Brownhill. Without that, she would have died in six months.

When she was first arrested, by Inspector Foster of Knaresborough, May Brownhill was charged with 'wilfully and maliciously murdering her son'. She replied to the officer, 'Not maliciously – I simply put my boy to sleep.'

Self-Defence: Accidental Death – Just. The Irene Wray Story

The Second World War had been raging just a few months when a war of a very different kind was hideously present in the home of the Wrays, Norman and Irene, of Calverley.

Irene Wray, thirty-three, had a husband who was an arch-philanderer. He liked being with other women and he didn't want to be with the woman who truly loved him, his wife Irene. He was determined to leave home and when she was so desperate that she took out a gun to frighten him, it was with extreme nervousness and fear. For some reason, a statement had been made that she had pulled the trigger while her husband was looking through a mirror. What really happened was that she was never conscious of pulling the trigger at all.

But she was asked by Mr Justice Asquith to show the court how she actually held the gun that night. She held the gun with two triggers inside the trigger-guard and 'after two or three attempts' she pulled back the trigger. This was a gargantuan

Hebden Bridge. The author

effort of will for her and she collapsed after handing the gun back to the attendant.

Irene had gone to her family doctor after the killing and said, 'I have shot my husband in the back of the neck. He will be dead by the time you get there.' He died in hospital, and nothing could save him. What emerged from the defence case was that her husband ill-treated Irene and he spent time with other women. There were accounts of him being cruel to her and to their child.

Mr Justice Asquith summed up by making everything clear-cut. He said: 'There is no question of a manslaughter verdict or indeed of guilty but insane.' The only choice open to the jury was to return a verdict of guilty or not guilty. Irene Wray was found not guilty and walked free, to a round of loud applause from the public.

Within only a week of these events, Edna Hague of Sheffield, was also acquitted but this time by a halt to proceedings as the jury announced that they did not want to hear any more evidence. Edna Hague was charged with the manslaughter of her father, Alfred. The man had given a dying oath that he had stumbled and fallen on a knife. He had actually violently attacked Edna twice on the night of his death. Such was the intensity of the narrative of that violence that the jury had heard enough and the accused was released. Judge Lewis said: 'You did what anybody would do if they were in fear of their lives. You are instantly discharged.'

Diminished Responsibility: Shirley Campbell (1957)

The new law had just been passed, sorting out the difficult issue of diminished responsibility, when twenty-one-year-old Susan Campbell faced a murder charge. Campbell, a Keighley mill-worker, was babysitting seventeen-month-old Susan Pickles of Worth Village when the baby-sitter strangled her charge. Was she a murderer or was it manslaughter? Three days before this trial the legislation came into force.

Under section two of the Homicide Act (1957), if an accused person is considered to be mentally abnormal to such an extent that this substantially impairs the sense of responsibility, then a reduced charge of manslaughter applies. Mr Drabble, for the prosecution, pointed out the guidelines, stressing the point was about 'mental abnormality' but not 'insanity'. The evidence pointed to Howard's diminished responsibility applying here.

The defence lawyer, Geoffrey Veale, told the jury: 'It may be that you are the first jury ever to consider this kind of question.' He was quite right.

Reprieve: The Cruelty of Two Sheffield Parents (1953)

A reprieve usually occurs in a context in which there is a certain level of public sympathy for the perpetrator of a murder, and examples of that are easy to find. But what about a case of extreme cruelty in which mercy is given? That was the case with Patrick and Beatrice Conroy in Sheffield fifty-three years ago. They were very fortunate to escape the noose. What they did was brutalise and kill their baby, a child who was found in a sack in a cellar with fourteen stab wounds to his body. Mr Justice Stable said that they were guilty of concealing a birth and infanticide. That amounted to a murder charge for both of them and they were sentenced to death.

That was on 4 December. But an appeal followed, based on the slenderest of causes – a misdirection by the judge at the trial. Their counsel argued that Mr Justice Glyn-Jones should have tried the two separately. But all this was nothing of any consequence and the appeal was quashed. They were to hang at Strangeways.

The appeal was dismissed on 19 January 1954 and they were to hang, as the rule went, after two Sundays had passed. But then came the reprieve on 1 February.

Reprieve: Elizabeth Rhodes – Self-Defence?

In the courtroom in 1933, Leeds Assizes was buzzing with debate and discussion. Had Elizabeth Rhodes of Hebden Bridge killed spontaneously in the heat of an argument? Had she actually killed while defending herself? Or was she a murderer?

The Rhodes had had many years of unhappiness in their marriage. On the night of his death, something happened that had made 'the worm turn' – Elisabeth Rhodes was Irish and as the Irish national anthem was to be played on radio. Samuel Rhodes turned it off. The quarrel had become worse and worse as time wore on, and her testimony was that he had said that the next time they had a disagreement he would 'finish her'. But the fact at the centre of the trial was that Samuel had been killed by a single hammer blow to his head. It was a long-shafted hammer, very heavy. One blow would have been all that was needed.

What emerged was the familiar question of whether or not Elisabeth had planned and had the intention of killing Samuel, or whether it was a decision taken on the instant, under duress. The defence, led by Paley Scott, was that she killed her husband in self- defence. But the prosecution argued that she had killed him as he lay asleep in bed, not as he came at her with intent to do her harm.

It was a case of whether or not the jury would be convinced by the way Mrs Rhodes put her statements and gave her reasons for the action. They decided that she intended to kill him and that she murdered him in his bed. From there the case went to the court of appeal.

Mr Justices Swift, Branson and MacKinnon heard the case at appeal, which was based on the argument that several pieces of evidence about Mrs Rhodes' likely behaviour that night were not fully dealt with in the judge's summing up – so that would influence the decision of the jury.

In the appeal court, it was reinforced that Elisabeth Rhodes had tried to take her own life on five occasions during her life with her husband and his brutal regime of abuse and threats. She had even thrown herself into a canal at one point. But the appeal decided that the provocation, including this element of stress and mental derangement, had been fully discussed at the first trial. It must have been a very tense moment in that court, because the decision was going to decide whether or not the woman would hang.

The judges decided that there was no need to interfere with the initial judgement. The only hope then was an appeal for mercy. A petition was circulated during the next weeks, and as the rule that three Sundays had to pass between sentence and execution was in force, there was time for this. The MP for Sowerby Bridge, Mr S McCorquedale, presented the petition to the Home Secretary. On 23 August, *The Times* reported that Mrs Rhodes was in Strangeways Prison, Manchester, awaiting execution, but that the petition was under consideration. The Vicar of Halifax was one of the most well-known signatories.

The repeal came and there were surely some very audible sighs of relief in that prison cell and across her home territory. Forty-one-year-old Elisabeth Rhodes had escaped the noose.

The Scaffold

In 1924, Earl Russell put forward a plan to replace hanging with gas-poisoning. He thought that this would be a more humane method of execution, arguing that 'poisoning would cause less unpleasant anticipation, and there would be no disagreeable spectacle for the onlookers if coal gas were introduced at night into the condemned cell when the convicted person were asleep'. But hanging had almost always been the preferred method of death and at that time. Professor Harvey Littlejohn of Edinburgh University, replied to Earl Russell by saying that 'death by hanging was absolutely instantaneous'. That was certainly not true, and it had not always been so.

Calcraft's business display. Author's collection

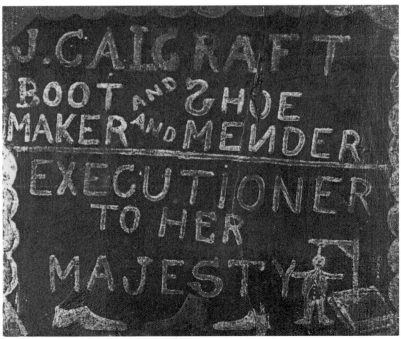

The gallows and rope method goes back a very long way. In early medieval times the gallows was a structure of two upright posts and a cross-beam. This would involve the use of a long pole so that several victims could climb a ladder and stand with the noose around their necks – to die almost simultaneously. Of course, in those early days before more professional hangmen, friends and relatives would pull on the victim's legs to hasten their death. In York, the Tyburn was a triple tree structure on the Knavesmire, so some of the women in this book would have met their end there: a triangular set of posts with the victim standing in a cart beneath and the rope slung over one of the beams.

Someone like the murderous Mrs Barber was destined to experience the 'short drop', which was decidedly inhumane. She would have fallen only three or four feet and taken several minutes to die. Of course, everything depended on the weight of the victim. William Marwood developed the more humane long drop and did more specific calculations to quicken the death.

Hangings were public until 1868, and the last of these in Yorkshire was that of Ursula Lofthouse in 1835. After 1868 hangings were done behind the gaol walls and, at long last, the disgusting public spectacle of a hanging as an entertainment for the crowds came to an end. Where women were concerned, there were several very widely discussed cases into the twentieth century, including the hanging of Ethel Major at Hull Prison in 1934 and, of course, that of Ruth Ellis, the last woman to be hanged in Britain, in 1955. She shot her lover in a situation of what in France would have been a *crime passionel*, but there was no such concept in English criminal law.

The whole ritual of hanging was extremely terrifying to most victims and was designed to instil fear, mainly through the awful anticipation of what suffering was to come. After Marwood developed the more humane long drop, most hang-men gained a sense of professional pride involved in making a person's last moments towards death as swift as possible. It was considered very professional, in the twentieth century, to be able to despatch the murderer in a time somewhere between seven and twelve seconds. But the entire process of hanging a woman, from the death cell to the pinioning and the pulling of

DIANA WITHOUT GLAMOUR
Outstanding in 'most gruesome' film

BRITAIN last night presented the most harrowing picture so far shown at the 1956 Cannes film festival when "Yield to the Night," in which Diana Dors plays a murderess in the condemned cell, was given its world premiere.

The blonde star was cheered by 3,000 people as she left the floodlit Festival Palace in her turquoise car matching her turquoise mink stole and sequin-studded evening gown.

She told reporters: "This is the part I have been waiting for, and it has taken me nearly 10 years to achieve it."

Film experts among the

— as she appears in the film.

— as she is usually seen.

audience of 1,800 producers and technicians from 34 countries described the slowly unwinding tale of a

woman's last days under sentence of death in a British gaol as the most gruesome shown at Cannes.

CONTROVERSY

They said Miss Dors, cast as a woman torn between desire to justify her crime and fear of the price she must pay, gave the outstanding performance of a career so far built on her success as a glamour girl.

They also praised the sensitive acting of Yvonne Mitchell as a prison guard.

Members of the British film industry said the picture, to be shown in London soon, is bound to revive public controversy over capital punishment.

Contemporary piece on the film about a woman hanged, Yield to the Night.
Scunthorpe Evening Telegraph

the lever, was an additional stress on men at a time when perceptions of women were far more extremely 'feminine' than now, in the sense of their separateness and difference. That difference, embodied in the phrase 'the gentler sex', not only had a bearing on how a woman murdering someone was judged, but also on how hanging and its sombre rituals were understood.

The most dramatic example of this in Yorkshire is the case of Emily Swann, as discussed in Chapter 15, but surely the most horrendous was the case of Mary Lefley in Lincolnshire, who was certainly innocent, and the prison professionals knew it. The Bradford hangman, James Berry, had to have the woman virtually dragged to her death and his emotions were in turmoil, being in the heart of a tension between duty and human instinct to put right an injustice.

The sequence in the process of hanging meant that there was due consideration given to the subjects of repentance as well as retribution. In the days up to the abolition of public execution (1868), the general public knew all the elements in the hanging ritual and it was a public entertainment. The process was in this order, each with its interest for the media and the populace: trial, sentence, imprisonment, confession and repentance, suffering in anticipation of death, then the scaffold and the hanging. To put a woman through this was in some ways to test out whether or not she exhibited those 'male' attributes the Georgian and Victorian social worlds wanted to believe was an integral part of any woman killer – as that very concept seemed to go against nature. One York housewife noted in her diary that there were only two murder trials at York Assizes in one specific year: she was very disappointed.

The most powerful illustration of the added appeal of a woman being hanged is arguably in the case of Mary Bateman (Chapter 8). In 1809 the milieu of crime and punishment was barbarous in the extreme, though most capital crimes were commuted to transportation. Nevertheless, when Bateman was hanged at York, a massive crowd made a day excursion from Leeds, where she had committed her crime, and it was a public symbol of the general feeling of suitable retribution for a gross abnormality in nature that a woman should kill by poison. Not only did they want to see her die: they wanted to be sure that the destiny of her corpse was the Leeds Infirmary dissection rooms.

The Workhouse
Workhouses were another type of prison with a different name. These were financed from the parish poor rate as the operation of the Poor Law, deriving from an Elizabethan statute, tried to keep people who were destitute within their parish. The logical conclusion was that the poor, with no means of support, would work for their keep in a place that was, to all intents and purposes, another place of punishment. Between 1723 and 1776, almost 2,000 workhouses were constructed in England, and by 1840 the new Poor Law of 1834 affected around thirteen million people in England.

As with a prison, workhouse men and women were separated and they could not communicate with each other. Visits, as with the prison system, were by arrangement only and had to be supervised. The entrapment that went on in these places worked this way: a pauper could apply to leave and he then left but if he could not support himself in the parish (which he could not) he had to leave. Then he was a criminal because he was a vagrant. This then became a huge problem and fuelled

Vagrants in the casual ward of a workhouse, from Mayhew's London. Author's collection

the prison population. As one man wrote of this situation in Devon: 'Numbers of sturdy beggars, particularly in summer, invade our farmhouses and cottages and in the absence of the men extort money from the women they find at home ...'.

Henry Mayhew, writing in his massive social survey of 1849–50, noted that the link between crime and vagrancy was very significant: 'Of the tide of crime which, like that of pestilence,

accompanies the stream of vagrants, there are strong and con-
clusive proofs' and the went on to describe a woman he met in
this situation, who said: 'I am now eighteen. My father was a
coloured man. He came over here as a sailor, I have heard, but I
never saw him; for my mother, who was a white woman, was
not married to him, but afterwards married a box-maker . . .'. In
other words, the roots of her predicament were in the rootless
life and that sprang from a broken family and so on.

These various destinations of women murderers show the
amazing variety of workings of the law over the centuries, and
they show that women in Yorkshire, when pushed and pres-
sured to kill, have been example of the universals of murder:
jealousy, satisfaction, sense of justice and greed being the
motives. The saddest cases have been those categories of mercy
killings and self-defence in contexts of sadistic brutality. The
range of destinations show that in the cases of women in
English society, from the early Georgian examples I have discussed (in Beverley) through to the contentious homicides in
the later years of the last century, when a woman committed
an alleged murder, there were possibly a greater range of both
punishments and available options than there were for men.
This comes from the rather more direct and definable tendency
of the nature of make murder. A man usually take a life through
a jealous rage, a violent attack or a planned killing for gain.

In her important book on the subject of murder, *Murder and
its Motives* (1958), Fran Tennyson Jesse took a special interest
in the case of Constance Kent (in which two-year-old Francis
Kent was murdered), and at one point in her analysis she makes
a very telling comment: 'Also, Constance Kent's features were
of the regular and strongly marked variety – good looking
enough, bright, and perhaps too determined for the period in
which she lived'. In other words, there is a great deal of
irrationality in the public mind (and potentially also in the
average jury) when it comes to the image and appearance of
the female killer. Basically, they are easily mythologised and
demonised.

The ancient and persistent conviction that a woman killing
is 'against nature' is very deeply entrenched, and that point
underlies most of the case studies covered in this book. The

Victorian print of an accused murderess. Clifford Elmer

complex tension between how the state and the criminal justice system saw and dealt with female killers was always one in which the axis of justice and human nature held the interest. Perhaps Thomas Hardy was one of the most perceptive commentators on this and, his words at the end of *Tess of the D'Urbervilles* (1895), at which Tess is hanged, express this difficult conflict:

> *Upon the cornice of the tower a tall staff was fixed . . . A few minutes after the hour had struck something moved slowly up the staff, and extended itself upon the breeze. It was a black flag . . . .*

'Justice' was done and the President of the Immortals, in Aeschylean phrase, had ended his sport with Tess.

Recent decades have seen this issue very strongly, as a cartoon from the periodical, *The Idler* shows, from 1893. In the image, a judge protects the criminals and the figure of Justice is a woman. In late Victorian times, some elements in society were beginning to have their doubts about the fate of women caught up in the criminal law. Yet it was still to take over half a century to address the central issues of that bundle of fuddle and prejudice. After all, at the time of Hardy's writing and when the magazine printed that image, most women still did not have the vote and equal pay was a distant dream.

Announcement of Earl Russell's plans for 'humane execution' (1922). Daily Sketch

GAS-POISONING SENTENCES.

EARL'S PLAN FAILS TO CONVINCE.

HUMANE HANGING.

COAL gas poisoning for murderers instead of the present method of execution, as advocated by Earl Russell, has been condemned by Lord Justice Atkin.

Earl Russell contended that poisoning would cause less unpleasant anticipation, and there would be no disagreeable spectacle for the onlookers if coal gas were introduced at night into the condemned cell when the convicted person were asleep.

He made this proposal at a London meeting of the Medico-Legal Society, a body composed of doctors, lawyers, and criminologists, which gathers frequently to discuss various aspects of criminal matters.

MENTAL TORTURE.

The current number of the "Lancet" contains many comments of distinguished investigators upon this matter. Lord Justice Atkin, who presided at the meeting, considered that the proposal made by Earl Russell was objectionable, because if the prisoner did not know on which night he were to be poisoned he would lie awake many nights expecting death. If, however, he were forewarned he would certainly not sleep on the given night, and would be slowly suffocated while conscious.

Professor Harvey Littlejohn, of Edinburgh University, declared that death from hanging was absolutely instantaneous. He has been able to examine six recent cases of execution, and as a result contended that the method of hanging adopted in Britain was the most humane of all methods, the operation being performed expeditiously and painlessly, and it undoubtedly caused instant death.

He made an interesting comment on the beating of the heart after the drop had taken place. In most cases the heart continued to beat vigorously for ten minutes, but in one case the heart apparently stopped immediately.

MAHON'S BODY.

Sir Bernard Spilsbury, the famous pathologist, described in detail the examination he made of the body of Patrick Mahon, the Crumbles murderer, in which there were two dislocations of the spinal column.

The poison expert of the Home Office, Sir William Willcox, was another who said that hanging was a painless form of death, and that the hanged man became immediately unconscious, even if convulsive movements were observed afterwards.

For some time there has been public unrest with regard to the method of execution, and there is a feeling in this country that recently all has not been well.

To allay this feeling Lord Justice Atkin suggested that the authorities should provide for a post-mortem examination being made by competent persons, and that the results of the examinations should be published.

The presence of Sir Bernard Spilsbury at the inquest on Mahon and his evidence of the results of the execution appear to have been a step in that direction.

An Outline of Relevant Legislation

The following are merely some of the key dates and events in relation to criminal law and to the criminal justice system in England that relate to murder or to homicide generally where women are concerned in the legal process. Some of the events have simply been indicative of changes or a desire for change, either in the judiciary itself, in precedent or in the overall spirit of the age, as the winds of change began to stir.

1816 The first model prison was constructed at Millbank. A separate system for men and women was established. Plans for Armley Gaol, later in the century, clearly show the separate accommodation and exercise yards for male and female prisoners.

1823 The Judgement of Death Act meant that a judge need not pass a judgement of death on crimes other than murder (even though many of these were capital offences). This depended on the judge's opinion as to the accused's suitability for mercy – the mercy of the sovereign.

1829 Petty treason, in which a servant killed a master or a wife killed a husband, was converted into murder. This meant that no longer would a woman who murdered her husband be subject to death by burning, rather than death by hanging, which would have applied if a man killed his wife.

1832 Abolition of the death penalty for coining false money, house-breaking, sheep-stealing and horse-stealing.

1843 The McNaghten Rules. These put down guidelines on an insanity defence in murder cases. The defendant has to be shown to have been 'labouring under such defect of reason, from disease of the mind, as not to know the nature and the quality of the act he/she was doing ...'.

McNaghten had tried to kill Prime Minister Sir Robert Peel. At his trial he was found not guilty by reason of insanity, and by all three judges.

1853 The end of transportation to Tasmania (then known as Van Dieman's Land).

1861 The number of capital offences were reduced to just four, and the death penalty for attempted murder was abolished.

1873 The Court of Appeal was established. It was created with two divisions: the Criminal and the Civil, with the Lord Chief Justice as the President of the Criminal Division.

1879 The appointment of a Director of Public Prosecutions. These officials would take care of the proper procedure in the application of criminal proceedings.

1922 Infanticide was made a crime separate from murder. As James Avory Joyce has noted when commenting on that act, 'No fewer than sixty women had been sentenced to death, during seventeen years previous to 1922, for killing their new-born children – but they had all been reprieved by the Home Secretary, with one exception.'

1938 The Infanticide Act states that if a woman is to cause the death of her child by 'wilful act or omission' but does so when it can be demonstrated that, at the time, the balance of her mind was 'by her not having recovered from the effect of giving birth to the child', then the offence would be infanticide, not murder, and so would be a variety of manslaughter.

1951 The Witchcraft Act was abolished, despite the fact that the last supposed witch was executed at Exeter in 1682.

1957 The Homicide Act made clear some guidelines on diminished responsibility. The line of thought here is that a person was suffering from such abnormality of mind when the homicide was committed that his or her judgement was substantially impaired. The conviction becomes manslaughter.

1965 The Murder (Abolition of Death Penalty) Act brought the end of the hanging of convicted murderers. Life imprisonment was given as the alternative, or in the case of a person under eighteen, the punishment would be detention at Her Majesty's Pleasure. In 1956, the House of Lords had rejected what was known as the Sydney Silverman Bill, aiming to abolish the death penalty for a trial period. It was defeated by 368 to 95 votes.

Sources and Bibliography

I. Books

Abbot, Geoffrey, *Lipstick on the Noose*, Summersdale, 2003.

Archer, William, *Old Time Punishments*, Andrews, 1890.

Barnard, Sylvia, *Viewing the Breathless Corpse: Coroners and Inquests in Victorian Leeds*, Words@Woodmere, 2001.

Bateson, Charles, *The Convict Ships 1787–1868*, Branston, 1959.

Bellamy, John, *Robin Hood: An Enquiry*, Crook Helm, 1985.

Bentley, David, *The Sheffield Hanged 1750–1864*, Alistair Lofthouse, 2004.

Bentley, David, *The Sheffield Murders 1865–1965*, Alistair Lofthouse, 2003.

Birkett, Sir Norman (ed.), *The Newgate Calendar*, Folio Society, 1951.

Brabin, Angela, *The Black Widows of Liverpool*, Palatine Books, 2003.

Briggs, Asa, *Victorian Cities*, Penguin, 1968.

Burnley, J, *West Riding Sketches*, Hodder and Stoughton, 1875.

Clarke, A A, *The Groaning Gallows*, Arton, 1994.

Clarke, A A, *Killers at Large*, Arton, 1996.

Cook, Chris, *Britain in the Nineteenth Century 1815–1914*, Routledge, 2005.

Cooper, T P, *The History of the Castle of York*, Elliot Stock, 1911.

Cyriax, Oliver, *The Penguin Encyclopaedia of Crime*, Penguin, 1996.

D'Cruze, et alia, *Murder*, Willan Publishing, 2006.

D'Cruze, Shani, *Crimes of Outrage: Sex, Violence and the Victorian Working Women*, UCL Press, 1998.

Davies, Owen, *Murder, Magic and Madness: The Victorian Trials of Dove and the Wizard*, Pearson, 2005.

Deans, R Storry, *Notable Trials: Romances of the Law Courts*, Cassell, 1909.

Dernet, J, *Beverley Borough Records 1575–1821*, Beverley, 1933.

Donaldson, William, *Rogues, Villains and Eccentrics*, Phoenix, 2002.

Eddleston, John J, *The Encyclopaedia of Executions*, Blake.

Emsley, Clive, *Crime and Society in England, 1750–1900*, Pearson, 1997.

Ellis, John, *Diary of a Hangman*, True Crime Library, 1997.

Evans, Stewart P, *Executioner: The Chronicles of James Berry Victorian Hangman*, Sutton, 2004.

Friar Stephen, *The Sutton Companion to Local History*, Sutton, 2001.

Gaute, J H H and Odell, Robin, *The Murderer's Who's Who: 150 Years of Notorious Murder Cases*, Pan Books, 1979.

Hale, Leslie, *Hanged in Error*, Penguin, 1961.

Hammerton, A James, *Cruelty and Companionship: Conflict in Nineteenth Century Married Life*, Routledge, 1992.

Hardy, Thomas, *Tess of the D'Urbervilles* (1895), Penguin, 1978.

Harrison, Paul, *Yorkshire Murders*, Countryside Books, 1992.

Hawkins, Henry, *Reminiscences*, Nelson, 1904.

History, Topography and Directory of East Yorkshire, Preston Barbour, 1892.

Huggett, Rene and Berry, Paul, *Daughters of Cain: The Story of the Women Executed since Edith Thompson in 1923*, Allen and Unwin, 1956.

Isaacs, Rufus, *Rufus Isaacs, First Marquis of Reading*, Hutchinson, 1942.

Jesse, F Tennyson, *Murder and its Motives*, Pan, 1958.

Jones, Ann, *Women Who Kill*, Gollancz, 1991.

Joyce, James Avery, *Justice at Work: The Human Side of the Law*, Pan, 1955.

Knight, Stephen and Uhlgren, Thomas, *Robin Hood: A Mythic Biography*, Cornell University Press, 2003.

Knight, Stephen, *Robin Hood and Other Outlaw Tales*, TEAMS, Michigan, 1997.

Kray, Kate *Killers: Britain's Deadliest Murderers Tell Their Story*, Blake, 2004.

Lane, Brian, *The Encyclopaedia of Forensic Science*, Headline, 1992.

Leman, Thomas Rede, *York Castle*, J Saunders, 1829.

McMahon, K A, *Beverley*, Dalesman Books, 1973.

Mayhew Henry, *London Labour and the London Poor (1849–50)*, Penguin, 1985.

Moorhouse, Geoffrey, *The Pilgrimage of Grace*, Phoenix, 2002.

Nield, Basil, *Farewell to the Assizes*, Garnstone Press, 1972.

Norris, Joel, *Serial Killers: The Growing Menace*, Arrow Books, 1990.

Palmer, Roy (ed.), *A Touch on the Times: Songs of Social Change 1770–1914*, Penguin, 1970.

Porter, Roy, *Madness: A Brief History*, Oxford, 2002.

Rees, Sian, *The Floating Brothel*, Review, 2001.

Ridley, Jasper, *A Brief History of the Tudor Age*, Robinson, 2002.

Satchell, Tony, *For Better or Worse: Convict Lives Shaped by Transportation*, Satchell, 2003.

Sharpe, James, *Witchcraft in Early Modern England*, Pearson, 2001.

Smith, Sir Sydney, *Mostly Murder*, Odhams, 1959.

Steinbach, Susan, *Women in England 1760–1914*, Orion, 2005.

Thornton, David, *Leeds, The Story of a City*, Fort Publishing, 2002.

Tibballs, Geoff, *The Murder Guide to Great Britain*, Boxtree, 1994.

Tobias, J J, *Crime and Industrial Society in the Nineteenth Century*, Penguin, 1972.

Twyford A W and Griffiths, Major Arthur, *Records of York Castle*, Griffith and Farron, 1888.

Walker, Peter N, *Murders and Mysteries from the Yorkshire Dales*, Hale, 1991.

Watson, Katherine, *Poisoned Lives: English Poisoners and their Victims*, Hambledon, 2004.

Whitworth, Alan, *Foul Deeds and Suspicious Deaths on the Yorkshire Coast*, Wharncliffe Books, 2001.

Wiener, Martin J *Reconstructing the Criminal: Culture, Law and Policy in England, 1830–1914*, Cambridge University Press, 1994.

Woodley, Mick (ed.), *Osborn's Concise Law Dictionary*, Thomson, 2005.

Yorkshire Star Chamber Proceedings, Vol. II, 1920.

Young, Angus, *Murders of Hull*, Quality/Hull Daily Mail, 1995.

Young, Angus, *More Murders of Hull*, Quality/Hull Daily Mail, 1995.

II. Journals, newspapers and periodicals

Annual Register.

The Daily Express.

Household Narrative.

Hull Daily Mail.

Journal of Social History.

Knelman, Judith, 'Women Murderers in Victorian Britain', *History Today*, August 1998 pp. 9–14.

The Journal of the Police History Society.

The Times Digital Archive.

True Crime Magazine.

Yorkshire Notes and Queries.

Yorkshire Post.

III. Archive and internet sites

Court of Criminal Appeal Records, 1927.

East Riding of Yorkshire Archives refs: Quarter Sessions Records: QSF/364/B/1, QSF/364/C/2, QST /18/1, QST/18/3, QSF/364/c/4, QSF/246/C/12, QSF/301/D/15.

Regina v Pendelton, Court of Appeal from http://www.publications.parliament (explanation of the history of the court of appeal), December 2001.

www.dg.petch.btinternet.co.uk (This is the main source for the Dry case, Driffield).

www.murderfiles.com

Index

Places